YOUR MOVE TO THE COUNTRY

Books by Dennis Ogden

Around the Next Bend
Off the Beaten Path
Last Children of Earth
Your Move to the Country

YOUR MOVE TO THE COUNTRY

An Escape from the City

Dennis Ogden

15-OGDE

To order additional copies of this book, contact:
Xlibris Corporation
1-888-7-XLIBRIS
www.Xlibris.com
Orders@Xlibris.com

CONTENTS

This book is dedicated to the generations of families who have striven to survive in the sometimes hostile environment of rural America. They crossed the mountains and the plains in search of a new way of life. But for their determination, where would we be now?

PREAMBLE

A Parable To Ponder

One day a very wealthy father took his son on a trip to the country for the sole purpose of showing his son how it was to be poor. They spent a few days on a farm of what could be considered a very poor family. After their return trip, the father asked his son how he liked the trip

"It was great, Dad," his son replied.

Did you see how poor people can be?" the father asked.

"Oh Yeah,' said the son.

"So what did you learn from the trip?" asked the father.

The son answered, "I saw that we have one dog and they had four. We have a pool that reaches to the middle of our garden and they have a creek that has no end. We have imported lanterns in our garden and they have the stars at night. We have a small piece of land to live on and they have fields that go beyond our sight. We have servants who serve us, but they serve others. We buy our food, but they grow theirs. We have walls around our property to protect us, they have friends to protect them.

The boy's father was speechless.

Then his son added, "It showed me how poor we are."

CHAPTER ONE

THAT PRIMITIVE URGE

Deep in the psyche of all of us is the primitive urge to be self sufficient—for the man the primeval task of hunting for the meat for his family's table and for the woman the age old task of gathering and harvesting nature's bounty. Our ancestors spent time teaching their children the skills necessary to survive a harsh environment. For perhaps two million years mankind lived the hunter/gatherer lifestyle. It was only some seven thousand years ago that we started to settle into communities in the fertile valleys of the near east—to gather in small hamlets, then larger villages, towns, and finally the big cities that now dominate our civilization.

But that primitive urge is still there. We sit at our desks in the big cities and daydream of that homestead that would free us from the daily grind. The vision of the cattle peacefully grazing on our own land. Bountiful harvests of fruit and vegetables—free of pesticides and chemical contamination. To sit by a warm wood fire in the evening while planning on the next day's activities without the interference of a demanding boss.

An idyllic dream—maybe. Can it be accomplished in this day and age?—again maybe. Why maybe? Because it takes planning, knowledge, some money, and lots of hard work to accomplish that which our ancestors seemed to do almost instinctively.

In this short book I will try to cover all the aspects of such a move from a controlled city environment to an environment over which you yourself have some, and perhaps complete, control.

The big move and change of lifestyle to the country living can be for a variety of reasons:

A simple desire to leave the city for more peaceful retirement years.

A desire to supplement some other source of income or pension.

A desire to leave the crime, noise, and stress of the city while still doing the same non-agricultural type of work in which you have already acquired skills—but do it in a better environment.

A wish to take on another occupation out of the city, again non-agricultural. This could be for wages or some type of self employment.

And perhaps the hardest to accomplish, a desire to assume a full time occupation as some type of farmer/rancher.

In all of these changes of lifestyle there are a number of factors that have to be considered. Such factors as schooling for children; availability of medical care; cost of living; funds available to finance the move; cost of land and/or housing; certain cultural changes; and, of great importance, just where to move. These and other considerations will comprise the bulk of this little book.

My qualifications to expound in this didactic manner? My wife and I have done it! I retired from the really highly controlled life of 20 years in the US Army and with my wife and three teenagers moved to 40 acres of sage brush in north eastern Washington state— there to build a self sufficient homestead. Prior to the Army, while young and single, I made my living on a hundred acre farm in Ontario, Canada, raising cattle, pigs and chickens. My wife and I have lived in Central America for three years working with, and advising, subsistence level farmers on farming methods. In a non-farming context we have built and now operate a Recreational Vehicle Park in the Arizona desert. These three rural occupations can be taken as examples of full time farming, farming to supplement a pension, and a rural occupation that is not agricultural.

CHAPTER TWO

THE WHO, WHERE, WHY AND WHEN?

The who?: Living deep in the country is not for everyone. If you or a member of your family need daily, or even frequent, medical attention, the simple economics and time required for long trips to a town can be not just a problem, but could be medically dangerous.

Money plays its part. Groceries at small town grocery stores tend to be more expensive than in the city. Gasoline costs more. Nothing that is manufactured or trucked in is cheaper in the country. Utilities are just as high and your phone bill will be almost all long distance calls. Vehicle wear and tear and fuel cost are greater due to poorer roads and higher mileage that is common for rural dwellers. Put very simply, the cost of living in the country for basic necessities can be higher than it is in the city. To offset this, there is not the temptation to spend on non-essentials when the non-essentials are not immediately available!

If you will have to be working for somebody else for wages, it is important to note that rural wages are much less that city wages. Many occupations that pay quite reasonable wages in the city are paid at the minimum wage level in small towns and villages. And many jobs are part time jobs. This in spite of the higher cost of living. Be aware that, not only do jobs pay less wages in the country, there just are fewer jobs to be had.

The where?: If you have school age children there are other significant considerations. To illustrate, it is 72 miles from our present home to the nearest high school!—and 40 miles to an elementary school–a long time for children to be on a bus. In the northern states this presents a definite increase in exposure to the hazards of accidents in the winter ice and snow. Home schooling is a possibility–although I personally think that few parents are really qualified to be good teachers of their own children–and the children are deprived of the opportunity to socialize with their peers. To offset the negative aspects of long bus rides there is the fact that drugs and gang activities, while not completely absent, seem to be far less prevalent in the smaller rural schools.

If you are moving to the country to retire, then it makes sense to retire where you can enjoy the outdoors year round. This means, of course, Florida or the southwest. If you just MUST have some snow in the winter (something I personally don't understand) then there are some nice locations in the higher elevations of Arizona, Utah, Texas, New Mexico, and even, dare I say it? in California.

If, on the other hand, you will be working then the weather has to be taken into consideration. Construction and other outdoor types of work are pretty well all year around in the Sun Belt. In northern climates much of the available work is seasonal. Harvest work, while well paid, is very brief. Construction work is only in the warmer months.

Weather may also pay quite a significant part in health considerations. My arthritis, for example, was starting to cripple me in Washington but is now almost a thing of the past in the dry heat of Arizona.

To work at your present occupation, or to start a new one, it probably means moving near to a small town, or perhaps a medium or larger size one. Property located in close commuting distance to smaller towns can often be found at very reasonable prices. The implications of buying a residence in the country with the complications of rural utilities will be covered in a later chapter.

To farm, full time or part time, the major considerations are; cost of land, climate, soil quality, and water availability. We will cover these in some depth later.

In every case you can almost forget the opportunities to avail yourself of the cultural offerings that you have become used to having in the city. To go to the opera, the ballet, stage plays, art exhibits, even first run movies will often mean lots of planning–who will feed the chickens?–a long drive and perhaps even an overnight stay.

Offsetting the loss of cultural entertainment is the access to hunting, fishing, skiing, bird watching, hiking–and all the other outdoor activities not available in the city.

The Why? If you are already even considering moving to the country from the city or from the suburbs (they are not really country, now are they?) then you already have one or two reasons that have triggered the consideration. Let us then see if we can add some more reasons to move–and maybe some reasons not to move!

Healthy living is a much more achievable goal in the country. You can grow at least some of your own food, maybe most of it (there are no tea bag trees). Your home grown meat, vegetables and fruit will be free of insecticides, preservatives and chemical additives. Canning your own produce is not a hard skill to learn and a big deep freezer makes storing meat and vegetables easy.

Crime: Let there be no misunderstandings–there IS crime in the country, and while it is much less than in the cities, in fact it is growing faster in rural areas than anywhere else in the USA. But there is less crime, and it is crime of a different nature. Rural teenagers do have the deplorable habit of drive-by shooting–but it is usually not at people but at road signs and mail boxes. There is some drug crime but it is rare and it seems to be primarily limited to growing marijuana and drug labs making drugs to sell in the cities. There usually is not enough market for drug dealers to be common in rural areas. Of course, there is the usual domestic violence and other stress related crime that is now endemic in our society.

Pollution: Undoubtedly one of the benefits of country living is the air. Simply put, the fewer number of vehicles per square mile means fewer pollutants in the atmosphere. Rural water supplies are rarely chlorinated and this can be a plus or a minus. If the water supply is not contaminated then who needs chlorine in their drinking water? But in this day and age very few water supplies are as clean as nature intended. We ourselves get our water from a 900 feet deep well, but I still chlorinate our storage tank slightly–just to be sure. A point to note is that few rural water supplies are fluoridated and there seems to be no doubt that young children's teeth do benefit from fluoridation. If you have young children you might talk to their dentist about this.

Taxes: Taxes are lower, much lower in the country than in the city or the suburbs. But of course there is a reason for this–you get a whole lot less governmental services for your taxes. Our nearest police protection, the local deputy sheriff, is 40 miles away and takes 40-45 minutes to get here–if he is near a phone and not busy. Our nearest fire department and emergency medical services, all volunteer, are 6 miles away and can take up to an hour to assemble their people and call an ambulance or helicopter to get to our home. Our local library has perhaps three times as many books on their shelves as I have on mine–though to be fair they can get books from other libraries on inter-library loans. Our roads are terrible and will probably stay that way forever. We have to drive 6 miles to pick up our mail at an inadequate contract post office. As mentioned earlier our high school is 72 miles away–the same distance as the community college. The nearest 4-year college in our state is almost 200 miles away. Of course is you don't want or need any of these services then the lower taxes are just great.

Country folk make great neighbors–sometimes. Generally they initially resent any new neighbors for one good reason: City folk buying in the country will generally pay more for property than the local people would. The locals see this as a reason for their rising taxes–you have raised the assessed value of their property by paying more for yours than it is worth. Of course when the local people list their property for sale they ask more than it is worth, knowing some city sucker will probably pay the asking price, or close to it. The lesson to be learned here? Bargain hard–there is likely some reason somebody didn't buy it before you! Other than this resentment, country folk are used to helping each other out and will help you the same way—as long as you don't bring a superior city attitude with you—and they will expect you to be helpful when appropriate.

The When? The when covers two time periods: When in your life and what time of year.

When in your life is a decision that only you can make. You have to take a hard look at your finances. As I have said before, rural incomes (with the exception of the few large ranchers and farmers) tend to be lower than in the city. If you try to bring a large debt burden with you and try to carry it on a lower income, then this is a recipe for disaster. Take a hard look at those debts and see if they are appropriate for your contemplated new life style—do you really need a forty thousand dollar sport utility vehicle when a five thousand dollar used pick up truck would do just as well—one that you could maybe get for cash and eliminate a car payment. That SUV may be a prestige item in the city but in the country the bad roads are going to beat it to pieces and there is no one to impress when your nearest neighbor may be a mile away. The same with any other items you are making payments on—sell that fancy speed boat and get a five hundred dollar bass boat—the fish won't care! In other words evaluate all your financial affairs ready for a brand new life style—a happier, simpler one.

Take a look at your credit card situation. Ideally you take them all out of your wallet and cut them up with a pair of scissors—maybe keep just one (one with a low credit limit) locked away in a drawer for emergencies. Then settle down to paying off all the balances.

These financial decisions are hard ones to make and it may seem to you that I am exaggerating their importance. But until the day you can say, "I have no payments to make on anything!" you will not realize what an enormous relief it is to be free and clear of debt. My father, who was a very conservative man, used to say that paying interest voluntarily to some one else was like taking a pay cut voluntarily.

Of course, once you have decided on when and where in the country, you will probably have to assume new debts! A new mortgage, unless you have liquidated enough city assets to be free of a mortgage–what an ideal situation! I will have something to say in later chapters about purchases of such items as farm machinery and animals for those who might have an interest in them.

What time of year? A major factor for some is the start and end of the school year. Myself, I am an education fanatic–I can see no more important duty for a parent than their children's education. If you know where you are going, call the school and get dates of the start of the school year and coordinate it with the school your children are presently attending. One note of caution–if you have a mentally or physically handicapped child make a personal visit to the proposed new school and verify that they are capable of providing the services your child needs. If not, then find another, better, place to which to move.

The other consideration as to time of the year is the weather. If you plan to buy a home don't plan on moving there in the late fall or winter. There could be problems with the heating system, insulation of water pipes, flooding in the basement, etc. While it is a smart move to inspect a prospective new home in the very worst wet and cold weather–to check for roof leaks, basement leaks, frozen pipes etc., it may not be the best time to actually move in.

If you plan on buying land over and above just a house lot you must inspect it at the worst time of the year–during or right after heavy rains–if it is under water or subject to flooding at any time of the year then it is no use to you, unless you want to live in a houseboat! Besides which the seller will be more receptive to your offer if you and he are standing in a cold miserable rain looking at a dreary scene–a scene that is going to look more desirable and beautiful when the sun comes out!

CHAPTER THREE

THE PRACTICALITIES

OF COUNTRY LIVING

A home is more than just a roof over our heads. We of the western world have come to demand certain comforts above the bare necessities. You CAN live without electricity, but who wants to? A hand pump for water out in the yard on top of a well is adequate, but what a pain! A back house latrine facility was common many years ago—but it is highly inconvenient at three o'clock in the morning. My farm in Canada had all these outdated facilities for the first couple of years—no electricity, no water in the house or barn, a smelly outhouse. Never again! This is the 21st century and I (and you) want all the conveniences to which we have become accustomed. So let us look at each one in turn.

Electricity: Ideally it comes over wires from someplace else. Be aware that if you buy a place without electricity it can cost a lot to get hooked up to the system. For example it cost us over twenty-one thousand dollars to bring the electric lines into our RV Park—more than the land cost! Usually you get so many feet free (for us it was 400 feet), and then you pay for the rest at so much a foot.

A generator seems a practical solution at first glance. The problem is that they are quite expensive to buy and to operate and don't seem to last very long. Using one just, say, four hours a day you would be lucky to get six months of service out of it. Even the big diesel generators do not have a very good life expectancy. In

Vietnam we had, in our compound, enormous skid mounted die-sel generators to provide 24-hour electricity–they lasted about 6 months before having to be replaced.

Solar power is fast becoming a very viable possibility–at least in the Sun Belt. Currently the cost of enough large solar panels to be of real use is quite high–and of course they only work when the sun shines. The electricity can be stored in batteries for use at a later time.

Wind power has similar problems of unreliability–windmills only work when the wind blows. Again, the electricity can be stored in batteries for use at a later time.

Windmills are a very viable alternative for a water supply. Since they can pump into a water tank, and if the tank is big enough, a few days of no wind can be tolerated. They are also very useful in remote parts of a farm or ranch for watering animals. The major disadvantage is the cost of drilling a well out of which to pump the water. We will look at water supplies in a little more depth a little later.

You CAN live without electricity. Propane refrigerators are still made. Oil lamps can still be bought. You can pump your water by hand or with a windmill. Sit out in the car periodically and listen to the news on the car radio. There are battery powered radios, battery powered lap top computers, and lots of other battery powered gadgets. Try it for a few months–then talk to the power company about bringing in the power lines!

Water: The sources of water are quite varied. The problem in this day and age is pollution–both man made and natural pollu-tion. The purpose for which the water is wanted dictates what water sources are safely usable. It may seem a little harsh to say it, but animals do not need the same quality of water that we con-sider safe for humans. Wild animals drink out of puddles, stag-nant water, swamp water, etc., and don't seem to suffer any harm from it. Domestic animals fall in the same category. Sure it would be nice to give them crystal clear, pure water but they don't really need it. The same thing applies to irrigation water, it too doesn't have to be 100% pure to be safely usable. Let us look at water sources and their possible uses.

Ideally the easiest water supply is from some central water system where you just pay a monthly bill and get all the water you want at reasonable prices. This is rarely an option in a rural area.

A good, fairly deep well is the safest water supply for our purposes. Fairly deep because this eliminates the problems of contamination by surface water. A safe depth, in my opinion, is something over about sixty feet. A shallower well is OK for watering livestock but not for human use. Well drilling costs have remained remarkably stable over the last forty years. Currently you can expect to pay between fifteen and twenty dollars a foot for the drilling, plus about five dollars a foot for any part of the well that requires steel casing–usually the first twenty to forty feet, the same price range we paid over twenty years ago. This is for a six-inch diameter well. By this calculation a hundred foot deep well should normally cost somewhere between sixteen hundred to two thousand two hundred dollars to drill. You may have to pay a mileage fee for the transportation of the well drilling rig to your place. The well driller will NEVER guarantee you water! Where to drill is up to you–the driller will drill where you tell him too. He will drill to the depth at which he hits water or until you tell him to stop. He will want to be paid whether or not he hits water. And this brings up the question of "water witching" or water divining. Either you believe in it or you don't. I do. I have done it and successfully located water at usable depths. Even if you don't believe, what harm can it do to drill where the water diviner suggests rather than some other spot that has nothing to recommend it?

In addition to the cost of the well itself you will have the cost of the machinery to pump the water and the electricity to run the pump. The pumping machinery usually consists of a submersible pump; the piping down to the pump; a hydro-pneumatic storage tank at the well head to reduce the number of times the pump has to cut in; and some electrical/pressure controls to determine the water pressure being delivered. Total cost, depending on your needs for the house, any livestock, and any irrigation needs, is between a low of $600-$800 for a domestic only system (from Sears-Roebuck) to many thousands of dollars for a system capable of large scale irrigation. A decent system capable of handling the house, a couple of cows, a few pigs, a few dozen chickens, a reasonably large garden, and a small orchard can be put together for under two thousand dollars.

The capacity of the well is of some concern. The FHA and VA require that for them to finance a home the well must have a rated capacity of a minimum of four gallons per minute. This requirement can be waived down to ¾ of a gallon in some locations. Four gallons is really not an adequate supply for a house, let alone a garden and livestock. If you buy property with a well on it, be sure to look at the well drillers report, which should be filed in the county courthouse. Aim for a rock bottom minimum of ten gallons a minute and fifty is better! For really extensive irrigation a flow of over 100 gallons a minute is a minimum. Look where the well is located. Near to or surrounded by animal waste is bad if you are going to drink the water. In any case, if you buy property with a well on it or have a new well drilled, take a sample to a testing laboratory before use, and every year at least once, it is good insurance against possible problems from contamination.

Other sources of water fall way behind in desirability compared to the municipal water system and a good well.

In order of descending desirability they are: A running stream; a spring fed pond; a stream fed pond or lake with water flowing in and out; stagnant water/swamp water. Any one of these is adequate for livestock and irrigation. None are really suitable for human consumption without serious treatment. Unless you can go all the way up to the headwaters of a stream and be certain that it not being contaminated by insecticide, fertilizer, animal waste, or some other contaminant, you cannot be sure that it is safe to use. Even then, it can become contaminated after your inspection by such actions as aerial spraying of a variety of crop dusting chemicals, fire retardant chemicals by fire departments, illegal dumping of toxic wastes, etc.

Hauling water from some other source by vehicle is an option. In the area where we live in Arizona this is very common. Many people have a trailer mounted tank that they pull behind (usually) a pick up truck. They get their water at coin operated well heads, haul the water home and pump it in the tank that supplies the house. Normal consumption if you are not watering a garden or trees is around one thousand gallons a month for two people. The cost when you haul the water yourself is about two dollars to three dollars a month for a thousand gallons. You can have it delivered and pumped into your tank in our area for around fifteen dollars for a thousand gallons.

Sewage disposal: You have to live very close to a populated area to have the benefits of a connection to a sewer system. For most of us rural dwellers it becomes our own responsibility to provide our own private sewage system. And the words for that are: Septic Tank. The septic tank is perhaps one of the most useful and un-appreciated inventions of the twentieth century. This is the item that has all but eliminated the back house with its inconvenience, smell, and unsanitary operation and permitted the installation of clean, sanitary flush toilets, kitchen sinks, and showers in rural homes.

Septic tank operation is quite simple. Human waste, and in particular human feces, has a content of normal digestive bacteria. These bacteria, when flushed into a liquid holding septic tank, continue to break down the waste into a safe and sanitary liquid. This liquid is passed into lengths of perforated pipe, usually four inches in diameter, and it percolates into the soil. All these actions, in the tank and in the perforated pipe, take place out of sight under ground. There is no disagreeable odor or any sign of what is taking place out of sight. In your residence you can have all the conveniences that you have become accustomed to in the city— with the exception that a garbage disposal in the kitchen sink is not recommended for use with a septic tank. Used correctly a septic tank system with associated perforated pipe has an indefinite useful life. Correct use means that only the toilet, shower and kitchen liquid waste should go into the system. No solid material such as any plastic, metal, or other items that cannot be digested and broken down by the bacteria in the septic tank. No chlorine or other disinfectants that kill bacteria should go into the tank–and this includes no chlorine in the washing machine. Periodically the tank needs to be pumped out to remove any build up of solid material. How often this should be done is debatable and the recommendations vary for every couple of years up to every ten or so years. I like about three to four years. It costs around one hundred and fifty dollars to get the tank pumped out.

Septic tank installation is quite rigidly controlled by all local authorities to prevent contamination of water sources. They require a septic tank permit. A percolation test done by a specialist is always required to determine the absorption capability of the soil–this tells them how long the perforated pipe should be. The length of the pipe and the size of the tank are determined by the probable usage, usually calculated by the health departments on the number of bedrooms in the house. Septic tanks for domestic use used to start at about 750-gallon capacity. Most health departments have raised this to a minimum of 1200 gallons and up to 3000 gallons for multiple bedroom homes. Some very heavy clay soils all over the USA and some of the 'caliche" type soils of the southwest have such a poor absorption rate that a septic tank system permit will be denied. The alternative closed type systems that are available, while just as effective, are very expensive–they can cost up to twenty thousand dollars. If you are buying land with the intention to build, it can pay to have a percolation test done at your own expense (if the seller will not pay for it) before signing the purchase papers–or make the passing of the percolation test part of the offer to purchase–otherwise you could end up with that twenty thousand dollar expense.

Telephone: I am not familiar with the laws in all fifty states in respect to telephone service. Here in Arizona the state Public Utilities Commission has defined rules that protect your right to have access to phone service. Specifically: If the phone company cannot provide you with normal phone service within thirty days of your application for service they have to furnish you with a cellular phone and one hundred and fifty dollars worth of free service per month until the normal service is available. I would hope that other states have something similar–you will have to check that out for yourself.

Natural and manufactured gas: Natural gas or manufactured gas (propane) coming from a central gas company is never available in rural areas–the cost of the pipelines would be too high.

Propane gas in tanks is available. You can buy the tank–they vary from one hundred gallon capacity to several hundred and even thousands of gallons–or you can rent one on a yearly basis from the company that supplies the propane. Cost of the rental is quite reasonable–we pay forty dollars a year for a two hundred and fifty gallon tank and its associated gages and controls. The propane company comes out to refill the tank as it is needed. Propane cost is usually around the same price per gallon as regular gasoline. Usage will vary with the number of appliances you have that use the gas. For us, two people, we use about 400 gallons a year for cooking and heating the house. We have an electric hot water heater. Of course, living in Arizona, our heating bill in winter is not very high–we spend the difference trying to keep cool in summer!

One advantage of having a propane supply is the ability to cook on the stove during the frequent electrical power outages that plague us in the country.

Transportation: While not one of the home utilities, transportation must be considered when you live at some distance from even your closest neighbor.

THE vehicle of the rural dweller is the pickup truck. Sturdy, versatile and available, the pickup truck is invaluable when you have to bring home a dozen sheets of plywood, or three pigs, or a new water heater, or———whatever. It's OK to have a car, I guess, but a pickup truck is indispensable. In the north it has to be 4-

wheel drive–they use more fuel but will get you home through the snow or to town when a 2-wheel drive will not get through. With today's models that have extra size cabs and crew cabs you can carry six passengers and still load a few bags of cement or a refrigerator in the back. A new truck is nice–but after a few days it is a used truck! So look for a nice clean used pickup truck that has only been driven by an old lady to go to church once a week–it will last just as long as a new one and cost a whole lot less to buy.

CHAPTER FOUR

Your Country Home

You probably have your own ideas on just what constitutes the ideal home. So, just a few comments.

Old farm houses: Older farm houses can sometimes be bought at what initially appear to be reasonable prices–and they cost a fortune to update to the standards that you are used to. The problems you can encounter can be daunting. The insulation will almost certainly be inadequate. The electrical wiring will probably be aluminum wire and totally inadequate for the electrical loads that you are likely to put on it. The water pipes will be corroded and in bad shape. The septic tank and associated system will be questionable. Dry rot and termites are always a possibility. The heating and cooling systems will probably need replacing. On the bright side you will likely get some full grown shade trees and other landscaping around the house. From this you have gathered that I do not recommend buying and renovating an older farm house–I have done it once–never again! A possibility of acquiring a nice home site could be buying a house that is obviously condemned and uninhabitable, or perhaps fire or storm damaged (and therefore cheap), tearing it down and replacing it with a new one. You would get the benefit of the trees and landscaping, an existing driveway, and perhaps some usable other farm buildings.

Building a home: This is an entirely separate subject. You already have opinions about what you like and anything I say is not likely to change them. Just be aware that costs for contractors can be higher in the country if the contractor, his workers and his machinery have to travel very far to get to your place. And the contractor/builder will charge more if there is no electricity on the site and he has to provide a generator. You will, of course, have your choice of design, material (wood, brick, adobe, etc.)

Mobile homes: In past years if you lived in "trailer" you had something wrong with you–"trailer park trash" was a common insult. Well folks, things have changed. The modern manufactured home matches, and in some respects exceeds, a contractor built home. There are strict building codes and inspections of manufactured homes that ensure their safety and compliance with all electrical, plumbing, and insulation codes. They are comfortable and well made.

Mobile home units come in three common widths: 12 foot, 14 foot and 16 foot. In just one or two states (Indiana is the only one I am sure of) 18 foot wide mobile homes are made and can be moved on public highways. Mobile home lengths range from a low of about 40 feet up to 80 feet. However you are not limited to a 16-foot width for your home. Most mobile homes sold today are "double-wide". Two units are brought to your land and attached together side by side. This can give you for example a 48 foot by 28 foot home using two 14-foot wide units. Two units in this fashion can be used to make up a home of over two thousand five hundred square feet using two 16'x80' units. You can have a three bedroom, 2 bath home with a fine big living room and kitchen, den, etc. And there are mobile homes made up of three units!

Prices for a new mobile home range from a low for a basic single wide 16'x50' at about thirty thousand dollars up to eighty thousand or more for a luxury home. Included in all prices are such items as carpets, drapes, refrigerator, cook stove, furnace, hot water heater, complete bathroom fixtures, kitchen fixtures, etc. Sometimes furniture is included–it looks nice but is usually not top quality. There is of course a range of quality in mobile homes. Some manufacturers just make better homes at higher prices.

You can have your mobile home installed above the ground (usually about two feet high) with a "skirting" around it and a set of steps up to the front door and the back door. This does give you some out of sight storage under the mobile home. The home is supported on a number of metal or concrete piers. Bear in mind that when you buy a new mobile home you usually do not buy the wheels and axles–they go back to the manufacturer to be used again. A nicer option, in my opinion, is to have the home installed at ground level. This is done by excavating a long wide trench about two feet deep before the home is delivered. The trench is 4 to 6 feet wider than the final home width, longer than the home and has a slope at one end so the unit(s) can be backed into place on its wheels. Then it is leveled with adjustable piers to be ground level, or just slightly above ground level and the wheels and axles removed. The "V" shaped front end(s) with the towing tongue(s) are removed, either by unbolting or by acetylene torch. You end up with an approximately two foot high crawl space under the home that gives you access to the plumbing and wiring if it should become necessary. A retaining wall is built around the home up to ground level and then backfilled with the excavated dirt. Now you have a ground level home with no front or back steps to–particularly nice for those who have trouble climbing steps or in a wheel chair.

Then, like the rest of us, you will likely almost immediately start building on additions–a work shop, a storage room, a sun porch, covered patio, etc.

You will have gathered, I think, that my recommendation for a new home in the country is a mobile home. Like many people, I never considered living in one and looked down my nose at the idea of ever having to live in one–well folks, we live in one now and love it. We had it built to our specifications and it is an extremely energy efficient and comfortable home.

Heating, cooling, insulating: The cheapest way to reduce the expense of cooling or heating a house is to have as much insulation as can be sensibly installed. In the summer the insulation keeps the cool in and the heat out, and in the winter just the reverse–it keep the heat in and the cold out.

In the city is was somebody else's job to worry about frozen pipes–now it is ours. Even here in the Arizona desert we have to insulate above ground pipes to prevent freezing and cracking at night. When I lived in Canada we had to insulate down to five feet deep in the ground–it freezes that far down in winter.

Heating your home: In the city, homes/apartments are heated by electricity, gas, or hot water (radiators). In many suburban homes there is also a fireplace–almost purely ornamental.

We can have all the same conventional heating systems in the country with one common and economical addition–wood heat.

Heating with wood has its advantages and disadvantages. If you own the trees then the cost is limited to the expense of cutting and splitting the wood. The chain saw and a splitting maul or mechanical log splitter are used. One word of caution: It is my opinion that there is no more dangerous tool in the world than the chain saw–it takes extreme and continuous care to use one safely. Ideally your fire wood should be one of the hardwoods–they burn hotter and cleaner. Wood from the evergreens, particularly pine wood, is a problem because of the rapidity with which it burns and the creosote and coal tar that are deposited in the chimney. Heavy deposits of creosote and coal tar can block the flow of smoke up the chimney and present an extreme fire hazard when they get on fire–and they will get on fire eventually. Chimneys should be cleaned at regular intervals and quite often when using softer woods.

To get usable heat from wood we do not use a fireplace–more heat goes up the chimney than stays in the room. A poorly de-signed fireplace can actually cool a room off more than it heats it. For heat, we burn wood in a wood stove. Wood stoves are heavy metal (usually) boxes with controls for the intake and exhaust of air and smoke. There is usually a shutter arrangement to let a controlled amount of air in to support the combustion of the wood and a damper flap in the chimney to control the exhausting gas and smoke.

There are some traditional designs of wood stoves–the com-monest being the Franklin stove. There are two basic types of stoves. Stoves designed for just heating are usually upright cylinders in a wide range of sizes. Many people keep a kettle of water simmering on top of the stove–not just to make tea or coffee but also to humidify the dry air you get with this type of heating. Not so common nowadays are cook stoves. Cook stoves have a fire box at one side and an oven right alongside it. There are usually six or eight lids on the surface that can be removed to put a cooking utensil directly on the heat. Above the stove is a long narrow warming oven–used to keep food warm, to dry out your wet gloves, etc.

To give you an idea of how much wood you might need, I can tell you that we used about eight cords of wood each winter to heat our quite small home in Eastern Washington. Winters in eastern Washington can be quite bitterly cold. A cord of wood is a stack of cut and spilt firewood four feet wide, eight feet long and four feet high–in other words a stack of wood 128 eight cubic feet in size.

Cooling your home: Homes in the city are cooled by air conditioners–and these can be used in the country also.

In the hot dry deserts of the southwest it the evaporative cooler that is more common. Commonly called "swamp coolers", the evaporative cooler is a manufactured metal unit that is set up so that incoming air passes through wetted material in such a manner that the air is moistened and cooled. They are much cheaper to buy than an air conditioner and much cheaper to operate. The only disadvantage to a swamp cooler is that they do not work too well when the humidity goes up.

CHAPTER FIVE

LET'S REVIEW

At this point in our move to the country let us recap and pull together some of the decisions we will be making.

We will have evaluated where we are going to live in terms of:

Medical care for everyone in the family

Schools for the children–perhaps even colleges?

Job availability

The weather

The cost of housing and/or land

The cost of living

Taxes, including property tax, sales tax, state income tax

Outdoor recreation opportunities

We have stimulated the children to be interested in getting involved in 4H activities or the FFA (Future Farmers of America). We ourselves have checked to see if there is a Grange (a fraternal order of farmers) in our area.

With all these considerations in mind we can move on to some of the harder decisions–just what are we going to do when we get there? At this juncture we can visualize ourselves sitting in our new home, comfortable, happy, but getting bored with just watching the television, and besides, the money is starting to get a bit low! So, on to growing stuff and raising animals.

CHAPTER SIX

THE SOIL AND GETTING IT TO YIELD A HARVEST

To grow good crops you need good soil. This may sound so elementary as to be childish, but it is a basic truth that cannot be ignored. If the soil is too acidic, or too alkaline, or too heavy and thick a clay, or too light a sand, or too rocky or gravelly, then it will not grow good crops. If the slopes are too steep and there is even a start of some erosion then the erosion will get worse if you disturb the surface. If the slopes are too steep it will be dangerous or impossible to operate farm machinery on them. If the land is too low and swampy it will be sour and difficult to work. Low and swampy land will dry up late in the spring and it will be hard to get crops to mature in time to harvest—and you will have lots of practice getting your tractor out of the mud when it gets bogged down.

To reap the full benefits of country living you must have more than just window boxes and landscaping. A garden is almost mandatory—and an orchard. There is probably not one item in the grocery stores in the way of fruit and vegetables that has not at some point been sprayed with one or more chemicals. Home grown means pure and wholesome food—for some people it may be for the first time in their lives.

Home grown produce usually does not look quite as pretty as the stuff in grocery stores. If it is grown organically without the use of toxic chemicals it will likely show some minor insect damage. If there is a problem with a lot of insect damage, there are some organic natural insecticides that are acceptable for your use. It is not within the scope of this book to go into the details of safe organic gardening–there are books by specialists to guide you in this matter. Just what crops you can grow will depend on the climate where you live and your soil. For those who want to take the trouble, a greenhouse can let you have fresh produce all year round–this also is a subject outside the scope of this book.

For a small to medium size garden it is not difficult to make *almost* any soil come up the standards that we want. Judicious use of manure and compost boxes will go a long way to turning a wasteland into a productive garden. If there is any livestock being raised in your location–milk cows, beef feed lots, horse racing stables, chicken ranches, pig farms, etc–they will be only too glad to give you all the manure that you want, free for the hauling. Commercial producers have chronic problems disposing of large quantities of manure–they may even deliver it!

For the serious gardener, *the compost pile*/box is a necessity. A useable compost box is made of any kind of material. It is about four feet square, three feet high, with no bottom or top. Into the compost box goes all the waste organic material–table scraps (less bones), outer cabbage leaves, cornhusks, coffee grounds, straw from the chicken house–any and all material that can be broken down by bacteria. You make multiple layers, in say 3-4 inch layers; organic waste, a little manure, some soil, water it a little every so often. Turn the contents completely over a couple of times (I like to have two boxes side by side and fork one into the other). In about six weeks in the heat of summer, a little longer in the spring and fall, you will have forty to fifty cubic feet of beautiful rich black organic compost to add to your garden–free!

For more than a kitchen garden and a dog or cat you must check on what the property is zoned for. It could be extremely frustrating to find your dream home, move in, and find that you can't keep a few chickens, or a pig, or a pony for the kids to ride because the local zoning laws don't permit it. The zoning regulations can be quite arbitrary since they have been implemented to protect the current residents and not newcomers. For example I have been told that there are counties in Oregon where you cannot raise a pig–other livestock is OK, but not pigs. In the wheat growing areas of eastern Washington state you will have problems trying to keep bee hives–the local wheat ranchers spray what amounts to the whole county for insects that harm the wheat and barley crops, and of course the insecticides they use kills bees–they don't want you suing them for your losses due to their spraying.

If it is your intention to grow more than just a kitchen garden then serious attention to the soil is essential. Talk to the local US Department of Agriculture extension agent about the soil conditions in the general area and in the specific area that interest you. If he has been the agent in that area for any length of time he will be able to give you some idea of the quality and quantity of local harvests, amount of fertilizer used to get those harvests, and maybe even something about local problems with insect pests.

CHAPTER SEVEN

KEEPING WHAT YOU HAVE RAISED

While it is a real joy to eat fresh produce right out of the garden in the spring and summer, we want to be able to eat the product of our labor all year round—and that means preserving what we have raised at the peak of its perfection. And this means learning the various methods of preservation. We will look very briefly at preserving the various meat products, but realistically we end up determining that freezing is the only practical way to preserve meat other than drying it into jerky. Meat can be canned, but doing it at home is a chancy business at best and we personally never found it to be satisfactory.

Canning: Most vegetables and fruit can be canned very successfully. Home canning involves using specially made glass canning jars and sealing type metal lids—do not try to use old jam jars, etc—they will not take the heat or seal properly.

The two modern basic methods of canning are pressure canning and water bath canning. One or the other can be used for all types of fruit and vegetables.

Pressure canning involves using a commercially made pressure canner and the correct glass jars and lids. There are several companies that make pressure canners and several that make jars and lids. Jars and lids are a commonly sold item in rural grocery stores. Pressure canners have tightly sealing covers that permit the contents inside to be brought up to temperatures higher that the normal 212°F that is the boiling temperature of water. The pressure inside is controlled by one of two methods. The older, and I think more dangerous method, uses a pressure gauge on top of the canner. You have to regulate the heat under the canner to get the desired pressure. The danger comes if the gauge loses it accuracy due to being damaged or being old and the pressure in the canner can get to be a lot higher than is safe–even to a bursting pressure. A better and safe type of pressure control is the type with a specially designed weighted piece of steel that sits on top of a vent in the lid. There is no gauge, but the metal piece has usually three holes than can be used to regulate the pressure–5 psi (pounds per square inch), 10 psi and 15 psi. Pressure canners come in several sizes–get the biggest one you can find–a big one costs no more to use and will can large (one quart) jars as well as the smaller jars (pint, half pint). The smaller canners will not handle quart jars–half pint, pint and quart are the commonest sizes you will be using with quarts being the most common. Currently the US Department of Agriculture, who put out some very informative pamphlets on this subject, does not recommend trying to can in one gallon jars or in a microwave oven.

The other method, much simpler, is the water bath method. This involves putting the glass jars completely under water in a large container and boiling the contents for a pre-determined time. Again, buy the biggest water bath canner you can find for the same reason as above. While this method is the easiest, it not suitable for some produce. It is necessary to know the acid content of the produce, particularly tomatoes, before deciding which method to use.

The companies that make the jars, the companies that make the canners, and the US Department of Agriculture will all give you all kinds of specific information to be used for each and any kind of produce that you can think of.

Other preservation methods: In years past there was a method used, and it is still used by some old time devotees. That method involves using melted paraffin wax and unsealed glass jars. This method was and is devoted primarily to preserving fruit jams and jellies. I don't like it myself–I think it leaves a slight paraffin taste to the food—but others don't seem to think so. Another less common method is drying. Fruits of all kinds can be dried for later use in a drier designed for this purpose. Dried fruit makes a tasty snack and can be re-hydrated for other uses such as pie making.

Another method of preservation for some items that has dropped out of use in the last few decades, but is coming back into use in the mid west, is the root cellar. Before the advent of the freezer and the refrigerator food was kept in the cool of the root cellar. Usually a type of cave dug back into a hill side with a door, or a kind of a basement hole under the house with a trapdoor entrance, such items as potatoes, rutabagas, turnips, carrots, etc. could be kept all through the winter with little or no deterioration. The reason they are coming back into some popularity is their secondary very valuable use—as a storm cellar when tornadoes threaten.

CHAPTER EIGHT

GROWING STUFF FOR SALE

Growing garden produce for sale–commonly called Market Gardening–can be a very profitable sideline or even a means of support.

Commercial production of garden produce and fruit requires two major things. Number one is good soil (see soil above) and number two is a market for the produce. Also required, of course, is the labor to tend the crops and the machinery to work the soil. Close access to water is essential.

The specific techniques of growing crops on a commercial scale is an occupation and skill beyond the scope of this book, however if you can grow produce for yourself in a personal garden and orchard there is no reason why you can't grow it for sale.

There are two basic methods of realizing an income from a market garden or orchard. Ideally, if you are located on a fairly busy highway, you can sell freshly harvested produce directly to the public from a roadside stand. Some jurisdictions require you to get a business license to sell directly to the public. Doing this lets you sell at the peak of maturity and freshness, thus getting a good price, and lets you get the profit that is skimmed off by the supermarkets and grocery stores–the entire sale price comes to you. You must note however that this is a seasonal income–unless you go into greenhouse production you won't have anything to sell at your stand when there is snow on the ground–to my mind yet another a good reason to live where it doesn't snow!

The second more common method, particularly if you get

into large volume production is selling to a retail store or a cannery. This can be a little hazardous. I saw one example of the problems that can be encountered when a neighbor of ours grew two acres of beautiful tomatoes and then couldn't find a buyer for them—after the neighbors took what they wanted the rest rotted in the field. The moral here when you are growing crops on this scale is to have your crop sold by a legal contract *before* you even plant it.

A third less common source of income is to process your crops yourself. For example, instead of selling tomatoes sell canned (bottled) spaghetti sauce—turn your strawberries into strawberry jam, etc. (see canning in chapter 7). This can be a useful supplement to fresh produce at your roadside stand. However, doing this on a large scale is moving into a whole new area that is outside of the scope of this book—we are interested in enjoying the outdoor life in the country, not starting a factory!

Tree farming: One possible source of a steady yearly income is tree farming—specifically Christmas tree farming.

There are a variety of species that are suitable: Scotch pine, spruce, fir, etc. Pick a variety that grows well wild in your part of the country

One advantage of this type of tree farming is the fact that the trees will do well in quite poor gravelly soil and do not require any irrigation.

They are grown for seven years and then harvested. They can be sold standing in the field, or cut and bundled ready for transport. There is particularly good money and personal satisfaction in selling them directly to the public—parents love to take their children to the country and let the kids pick out a tree to cut themselves.

Christmas trees are planted from seedlings about four to six inches tall at about three to four foot spacing in rows three to four feet apart. This can add up to over three thousand trees to the acre.

Other than a little cosmetic trimming every year to keep a desirable shape to the trees there is no work other than the planting and, seven years later, the harvesting. There are tax advantages to growing trees that do not apply to any other crops.

I had a friend in Canada who had exactly twenty-one acres of land. He planted three acres of seedlings by machine every year and harvested ten thousand trees for sale every year—a very nice part time business.

Of course, nowadays you might have to post an armed guard on the property from around the first of December until Christmas Day.

CHAPTER NINE

FARM MACHINERY

Here we need to look again at three levels of crop production—a kitchen garden (even quite large ones), commercial production of crops for sale in a market garden size operation and large scale farming. My father dug up and turned over his garden all his life with a garden fork—every spring. It took two or three long days of back breaking labor. I guess he enjoyed it? For a quite small garden (say twenty feet by twenty feet) this is still a very practical method of preparing the soil for planting—and it does really get you into that "back to the soil" mystique that may be your ambition. It gives you a chance to really see what kind of soil you have—how many rocks? Is it a good friable soil with plenty of organic humus? Is it too lumpy a clay and needs some organic matter to break up the clay? Is it too sandy and needs more organic matter to hold moisture? How deep is the topsoil and how porous is the subsoil? For the serious gardener these are all questions of deep interest. The first sentence in Chapter six above was "To grow good crops you need good soil"—if you are wanting to grow things to eat or to sell then the soil is more important than the color of the drapes in the house or how pretty the view is.

Nowadays few people dig up a garden with a garden fork—the flower beds maybe—but not the garden—it really is back breaking work. So, rototillers and garden tractors are the tools of the 21st century.

Rototillers: A rototiller is a gasoline powered, two-wheeled machine with two handles for the operator to hang on to and steer with. The operator walks behind the machine. The actual work in the soil is done by a mechanism that consists of a rotating shaft with curved metal strips attached that churns up the soil as it moves along. With the smaller, lighter models, the operator really does have to hang on and it seems like sometimes he is doing more work than the machine itself! Rototillers come with the wheels ahead of the rototilling part or behind it. A decent machine that is practical for more than a toy needs to be quite large and heavy, with the wheels ahead of the rototiller part. Rototillers are excellent for incorporating organic matter including crop residue and manure into the soil.

Garden tractors come in a range of sizes and prices. The simplest are two wheeled machines (there are a few rare one-wheeled machines) with two handles for you to hold on to while an implement of some type is between the wheels and your feet. They are powered by a small gasoline engine of usually three to five horsepower. They are quite satisfactory for cultivating between the rows during the growing season but are not usually powerful enough to plow the soils to any adequate depth. They can be used with a limited number of attachments–a plow blade, cultivator teeth, a hilling attachment for potatoes, etc.

Riding tractors: The next size up are riding tractors that come with four wheels and a more powerful motor of eight to twenty horsepower–at a much higher cost, around two thousand dollars and up (and up!). They will just barely plow to an adequate depth–you may have to do the same ground more than once to get the depth that you want. Riding tractors have a much wider variety of attachments and implements available including a small utility trailer, snow plow, spraying attachments, along with the usual cultivating, harrowing, and plowing tools. They are low enough and small enough to be very versatile in the orchard with the ability to go between quite low and close trees. The larger (20+ horsepower) models are quite adequate for up to two acres of market garden–if the soil is not too hard to work.

Larger tractors: New farm tractors are expensive–really

expensive! Eight thousand dollars and up for even quite small, inadequate farm tractors. Most are Japanese, and while they appear to be really nice tractors the prices asked are quite ridiculous. For smaller farms on a limited budget there is really only one tractor that is reasonably enough priced, available everywhere and can still be serviced with available parts. That tractor is the Ford 2N, 8N, and 9N series. These tractors were made in the thousands in the 1950s and sold for around seven hundred and fifty dollars brand new. Now, some forty-five years later they sell for over three thousand dollars used! A little heavy on gasoline–about a gallon an hour doing hard work–they are a highly reliable, powerful, and versatile machine. They are the only older tractor for which it is easy to get parts and service. They utilize a system called a "three point hitch" that allows the use of implements without wheels that are attached to the rear of the tractor and raised and lowered by the operator from his seat. At the rear of the tractor is an item called a "power take off"–this is a rotating drive shaft that is used to power equipment behind the tractor–such as a rototiller. Besides these specialized jobs the Ford tractor can do all of the regular pulling jobs–trailers, small tree stumps, pull a car out a ditch, etc. There probably isn't any kind of a job on the farm that can't be done with an attachment on an old Ford tractor–front end loader, snow plow, road grader, buck rake, etc, and etc.–the list is unending.

Other machinery: The range of farm machinery available for specialized work is amazing. The basic jobs can be broken down into several basic categories:

Tillage: Tillage is the old word for all the actions necessary to prepare the soil for seeding. This includes plowing (moldboard plowing, disk plowing, chisel plowing), which means turning the soil over; disk cultivating the plowed soil to break up clods; harrowing (spring tooth or spike tooth), which means leveling and smoothing the disked soil. The desired end result is a nice fine, but not powdery, soil ready for the crop to be planted. Ideally you have tilled your soil supplements, hopefully manure, into the soil.

Seeding: Seeding varies enormously with the size of the seed.

Potatoes at a half a pound each are significantly different from onion seed at thousands of seeds to the pound. There are specialized pieces of equipment for all sizes and types of seed. It is still practical in small areas to seed the smaller seeds the old fashioned way—by broadcasting the seed by hand. I have done this with alfalfa seed quite successfully, but it is not recommended for many crops—since there are no rows, you can't cultivate between the rows! Of course in the kitchen garden all seeding is done by hand in rows. For both the home garden and the market garden it is of benefit to plant several seedings at intervals in order to lengthen the period of harvest and have fresh produce for a longer time. A few crops can be started in the greenhouse, or even in trays and pots in the house, and transplanted into the garden when they have germinated and grown a little. This permits earlier maturity of crops if they get a start on growing before the outside weather is suitable. For market gardeners this is particularly important since the price of produce is at its highest for the first very early harvest and slumps quite deeply when the crop is available everywhere.

Cultivating: Cultivating after seeding is done to control weeds and keep the soil loose and friable. In the garden, cultivating is done by hand with a hoe. This is also the practice in many large market gardens. Doing it by hand means that fewer delicate growing plants are accidentally damaged. Cultivating by machine is only done with crops where the rows are spaced far enough apart for the tractor wheels to pass in between or straddle over the rows. This can be with such crops as corn, lettuce, cabbage, potatoes, etc. Tractor mounted cultivators have adjustable cultivator teeth to accommodate the various crop spacings.

Spraying: It is extremely difficult to grow any crops of produce or fruit on a commercial scale and do it organically. Either the crop is so damaged by insects that it is ruined or the product looks bad enough to be unfit to sell. It CAN be done—and organically certified produce brings much higher prices than normal—good luck! There are some quite nice backpack type sprayers good for a garden up to an in acre size—wear a mask! Any chemical that will kill insects is not going to do human beings any good—they are poison. For larger areas tractor mounted sprayers are used.

Harvest: Market garden produce being harvested for direct sale to the public is harvested by hand. This permits the selection of prime ripe produce over a period of time, particularly if plantings are staggered over a period of time. Crops harvested for sale in supermarkets and grocery stores are usually harvested a little before maturity in order for them to be in the store just as they get ripe. Harvesting of very large scale commercial crops requires expensive commercial equipment—a new 22 foot harvester combine for grain crops is between one hundred and two hundred thousand dollars depending on the make and model.

Large scale farming requires large expensive machinery and is outside the scope of this book. In the area where we lived in Washington State the local wheat farmers have farms valued up to and over one million dollars—and a million dollars worth of farm equipment. Machinery that wears out!

CHAPTER TEN

KEEPING LIVESTOCK

I have thought about writing a completely separate book about raising livestock–maybe in the future. It is a subject with a wide range of implications for any size of farm. What breeds are best for each particular use? What are the feed requirements of each animal? Where to get that feed? How to market and at what age or size? How to butcher for your own use–there are endless questions and no one person is expert enough to answer them all. This book is intended as an introduction to country life and is aimed at those who have perhaps been born and raised in the city or in the suburbs and maybe have only seen livestock on the other side of the fence while going down the freeway and looking through the car window. It is not intended to be a detailed primer with all the answers–I don't know all the answers–but they can be found in the books in the library and on the Internet.

It is necessary to have the right zoning classification to be able to keep livestock. There are places zoned so you can keep a saddle horse, but not a cow. There are places where you cannot keep a pig–but you can keep ten dogs!–and pigs don't bark.

All animals need a certain minimum of room to be healthy and grow. They need protection from the weather–rain, cold and the sun. They need fresh air and some sunshine, good food and reasonably clean water if they are to thrive. If you cannot provide these items then stay out of the livestock business–it's not fair to the animals and you will lose money trying to raise them in inadequate circumstances.

Barns and outbuildings: Most kinds of livestock need some type of protection from the weather–particularly young animals. For this we build barns.

Barns for animals can by built of many kinds of materials. European barns, and many on the east coast of the United States were built of stone. Hard work and time consuming to build. Stone barns tend to be dark, damp and poorly ventilated. If you have one be selective in the way you use it.

Many modern barns now being built are of the type called "pole barns". This construction involves digging a number of holes some five feet deep, standing heavy poles up in the holes, and using the poles as frame for the building. The poles are quite often power poles purchased from utility companies, either new or used. They come in a large variety of diameters and lengths (and prices). The poles are attached and stabilized to each other by heavy boards, usually in the 2 inch by 10 inch size. The roof is usually corrugated steel sheeting. The outer covering can be a variety of materials: plywood, metal sheeting, board lumber, etc. My preference is for board lumber. You can buy rough cut (un-planed) lumber in the one inch thickness quite reasonably priced. Placed edge to edge you get a wall that is not air tight. Having a wall with slight gaps gives you the ventilation you need for livestock. Damp, stagnant and humid air has killed far more animals than cold air. For very young livestock (chicks, baby pigs, etc) cover the lower four feet of the wall on the inside with plywood to keep any drafts from being directly on their bodies–there will still be adequate ventilation above.

Other outbuildings: Buildings are needed on the farm for a wide variety of purposes: machinery storage, work shops, grain storage, pump house, hay barns, etc.

As with animal barns, a variety of materials can be used. Many hay barns are built using the pole barn construction method above. The only difference is that buildings used to store hay do not usually have any walls but just a roof with a good overhang.

It's time now to look at each type of livestock

CHAPTER ELEVEN

POULTRY

Chickens: The first thing that comes to mind in poultry is chicken. Cheap to buy, easy to raise, quick to mature, easy to butcher and store. Useful birds that give eggs and meat. The chicken is the small farmers mainstay for his own use. We will look at turkeys (and ducks and geese) at the end of this section.

Nomenclature: Baby chickens are chicks. Females are hens. Males are roosters. Castrated males (quite rare nowadays) are capons.

Types of chickens: Chickens fall into three broad categories, the egg laying breeds, the meat breeds and the dual purpose breeds. The dual purpose breeds, the Rhode Island Reds, Barred Rocks, etc. are not raised commercially but are quite popular in the small farmer's flock of chickens. They don't lay quite as many eggs as the egg laying breeds–which are primarily White Leghorns–and don't give the quality of young fryers that you get from the meat breeds– which are primarily Cornish Crosses. The dual purpose breeds do make good stewing hens when their egg laying years (two or three years) are over and nice big roasting chickens if not allowed to get more than about eighteen months old–after one laying cycle.

Buying chickens: You can buy young laying hens, five months old and ready to start laying, at about five dollars each, but why do that when you can raise your own? Day old chicks are sold in batches of 25 to a box. If you wish you can buy them sexed–all male or all female. Male chicks in the egg laying breeds are very cheap since they don't put much meat on when compared to the meat breeds. The most expensive are the females in the egg laying breeds. Prices vary from a few cents each for rooster chicks to up to one dollar each for good laying chicks. Meat chickens are sold un-sexed (that is mixed sexes).

Raising chicks: The first thing to remember is cats and owls and skunks and rats all like baby chicks!–they find them to be a delicious snack. If you raise chicks where there is any possibility of any predator being present you must protect them with some chicken wire to keep the predators away.

Baby chicks are very sensitive to cold and drafts. They need to be indoors in a draft free area with carefully placed heat lamps over them to keep them at the right temperature. Use a one 250 watt red infrared heat lamp per 50 chicks in the cold weather with the base of the heat lamp at about eighteen inches from the floor. They need some kind of a circular surround at least a foot high to keep them from wandering away from the heat source–this surround can be just a cardboard ring in the first couple of weeks. Put a 3½ foot diameter circle for each batch of 25 chicks–or something equivalent for larger quantities at the rate of 3 chicks per square foot.

Before the arrival of the chicks–they sometimes come through the mail!–use a thermometer to make sure the temperature at the height of chicks' back (about 2½ inches) is exactly 95°F for the first week. If the chicks move away from the heat source then it is too hot, if they all huddle under it then it is too cold–raise or lower the heat lamp accordingly. After one week lower the temperature to 90°F by raising the heat lamp, and then by 5°F each week until the heat can be removed. As soon as possible move them to larger quarters–at least 1 square foot per bird until they are a couple of months old then two or three times as much—or more. Over-crowded chickens have a tendency to start cannibalizing each other.

On the day of arrival take each chick and dip the end of its beak into warm milk or water. Have lukewarm water in the water-ers. If they are late in arriving or have a long trip home to your place add a little sugar or corn syrup to make the mixture sweet to give them a quick boost of sugar energy.

Baby chicks can be raised on any surface that is not too slippery–they break their hips on slippery surfaces–coarse brown paper works–newspaper is OK. Do not use any sand, sawdust, etc. since the chicks will eat it instead of eating feed and will starve to death. Since they will be eating an easily digestible starter mash, they do not need any grit at first to help them digest the feed. For the first feeding and a few days after scatter some feed around on the floor until they learn where the feeders are–remember that they are babies!

Feed, clean water and dry footing should be available at all times. The food and water should be easily accessible without going out from under the heat source. The commercially made chick feeders and waterers are designed to stop the chicks from fouling the food and water with their droppings–they are cheap to buy, last for ever and are better than anything you can make yourself. The water gets dirty very quickly–it is cheap, change it often. Do not use any grit until they are about a week old, and then use fine #1 chick grit. Litter of peat moss, cottonseed, oat or rice hulls or dry sand can be added after the first few days

The chicks will talk to you! You should learn their language. If they huddle in a pile under the heat lamp and yeep, a loud chirp, they are cold. If they are too hot, they pant, with their beaks open, like a dog pants and crowd against the surround away from the heat. If they are contented, warm, and full of feed and water, they make a contented, quiet, peaceful chirp.

Chicken feed: Commercial chicken feed comes in three types: Starter feed, grower feed and layer feed–each contains a different protein level. Chicken feed is usually called 'mash"–in the old days it was common to feed wet mash to chickens. Laying hens will benefit from some waste garden produce—for example when you harvest a head of a cabbage give the hens the stalk and outer leaves to pick at.

Meat chickens: THE breed of chickens for meat is the Cornish

Cross. This breed grows at a fantastic rate. Given 24 hour access to food and water and 24 hour light they will reach 3½ pounds weight in six to seven weeks and five pounds by 9 weeks. It takes a special diet to do this—see below.

Feeding meat chickens: The Cornish Cross chickens are fed nothing but starter mash. It must be very close to each chicken—no chicken should be more than about eighteen inches from a feeder or waterer at any time. They will squat down next to a feeder and eat 24 hours a day—make sure the light stays on. Care of Cornish Cross while still chicks is the same as for laying hens. Do not provide roosts for these chickens. To reach about 3½ pounds each Cornish Cross will eat about 10 pounds of feed. The hens will be a little smaller than the roosters.

Laying hens: Chickens start laying at about five to five and half months of age. They do not need a rooster (male chicken) to be good egg producers. When a rooster mounts a hen and impregnates her, a small speck of blood shows up in the egg. Some people do like the appearance of an egg with that little speck of blood in it. Of course the eggs are not fertile if there is no rooster in with the chickens. This is only important if you want to raise chickens from your own eggs. More on this later.

They will lay for about 10 months and then go into a molt. They will lose some feathers and not lay for a couple of months—then start laying again at about 80% of the rate in the first laying cycle. They will repeat this cycle again after about 10 months, resuming laying at an even lower rate. By then it is certainly time to butcher them—they are full grown, eating a lot of feed and not laying a lot—they are just putting on fat.

Feeding and care of laying hens: Raising and keeping laying hens involves a different feeding regimen to that of meat chickens. The chicks are fed starter mash for the first month or so to give them a good start, and then they are switched to a grower mash. At five months of age they should be switched to a layer mash. The layer mash contains the vitamins and minerals to enable them to maintain high egg production while maintaining their health.

As mentioned earlier, chickens (in fact all birds) need some form of grit or gravel to help them digest what they eat. After the first few days the chickens should have fine chick grit available, changing it to the regular size grit when they are switched to the grower mash. At the time they are switched to layer mash they need one more item to be always available, and that is oyster shell– it goes to make good hard egg shells. The grits and oyster shell are very inexpensive and the birds do not use a lot–so be generous, change it if it gets dirty and make sure they never run out.

Housing laying hens: Chickens do better in clean draft free housing, with some ventilation. Once past a couple of months of age, like all birds, they prefer to roost above the ground rather than stay on the ground to sleep. Roosts can be staggered in an "A" frame style with several heights of roosts from one foot to six foot above the ground. Use round poles about one inch in diameter and allow about ten inches per bird.

Laying hens need a place to lay the eggs–like all birds, they like to lay in a nest of some type. For chickens we must furnish laying boxes at the rate of one box per five hens. The boxes should be away from bright lights–not in the dark, but in dim light. Each box is about a twelve inch cube, open only at one side, and with a two inch lip to prevent eggs from rolling out. The boxes should be up off the ground with a roost about four inches in front of the box. Rows of boxes can be stacked one above the other to a height of about five feet. There should be some clean straw in the box. Collect the eggs at least once a day.

Controlling egg production: Unfortunately it is a fact that not all your chickens will be good layers, and some may not lay at all. The low producers should be culled out for the pot. It is recommended that the flock be culled after two months of lay, after six months of lay, and if they are not sold, then culled again after the 10 months of lay. Birds culled on this schedule will be the best second year layers.

The indicators of good or poor egg production are the body condition and the pigmentation of certain parts of the bird. The birds should be examined in the afternoon or early evening after most of the day's eggs have been laid. Handle only the birds whose heads indicate that they might be non-layers (see below).

Examine the following: The comb and wattles (on the bird's head) should be full, smooth and bright red. A non-layer's comb and wattles are dull, dry and shriveled. The best birds have bright bulging eyes and rather smooth eyebrows. Birds with excessive fat due to non-laying have fat faces with sunken eyes and heavy eyebrows and forehead areas.

Also examine the vent and pubic bones. The vent (where the egg comes out) should be large, smooth, moist, and almost white. It is easy to visualize an egg coming out. The pubic bones (the two small bones either side of the vent) should be spread apart, thin and pliable. In non-layers these bones are thick and close together.

Study the pigmentation of the feet and legs. The skin in yellow skinned laying hens bleaches out—the shanks should be white, thin and flat. The shanks in non-layers are a yellow color, plump and round. A study of the shanks of the birds is the best single indicator of their production capacity at six months of lay.

Raising your own chicks: In earlier times nobody bought chicks—you raised your own chicks from your own eggs. Then, eighty or ninety years ago, the commercial producers got into the act. Producing eggs and chickens stopped being a farm sideline and became a business. Instead of flocks of laying chickens we got what amounts to egg and chicken factories. Now we have chicken ranches that count their birds in the millions. The end result is quite cheap chicken and eggs in the store—but they have no taste or flavor. We can do better.

One very unfortunate result of the commercialization of the chicken business is the selective breeding that has gone into developing the modern chicken. One of the things that has been bred out of today's chicken is the ability to go "broody" and hatch out a clutch of chicks. A mature one year old hen can comfortably sit about 12 eggs. Chickens nowadays will go broody, but will abandon the eggs after a few days—the brooding instinct has been bred out of them. It takes 21 days of continuously setting on the eggs by a nice warm hen for the chicks to hatch out. None of the common domestic breeds available will sit the eggs long enough to hatch them out. A few breeds of somewhat rare birds will still sit a clutch of eggs—bantam hens, some of the Asian exotic breeds, guinea hens. You can get ducks to sit the eggs long enough. I suppose in some way out farms back in the hills there are still hens that will hatch a clutch of eggs—if you can find some, buy them!—and keep raising them.

There are commercially made small electric and gas brooders that will hatch out eggs for you—give one a try, you might like the satisfaction of doing it all from start to finish.

Oh, and one final note, if she is going to lay eggs that will hatch that girl chicken needs a boy friend—a rooster is essential for fertile eggs. And don't forget that he provides a half of the heredity of the chicks—use a good, healthy rooster of an appropriate breed.

Butchering chickens: Our great, great, grandparents, while they were growing up saw their mother (or father) kill, pluck and clean perhaps hundreds of chickens for family dinners. Most of us today have had to learn how to this by being shown or reading a book—and it is something we are very reluctant to do. Some people, through perhaps excessive squeamishness, never can learn to do what has to be done. Few people actually enjoying killing things, though it doesn't seem to bother hunters and fishermen. It is a task that can be learned—a very necessary task on a farm with livestock. If you don't do it, then somebody else will do it, perhaps not as cleanly and humanely as you could. If you know which chickens you are going to kill, segregate them the night before and do not feed them—this gives the craw chance to empty out and makes it easier to dress them out. So, on to the somewhat unpleasant task of turning a chicken into a Sunday dinner.

There are at least five ways that I know of to kill a chicken (besides just shooting it!):

1. There is the old standby: A tree stump and a sharp axe. With this method it pays to have two nails driven into the tree stump or chopping block about one inch apart and sticking out about one and a half inches. While holding the chicken by the feet with one hand, put the chicken's neck between the nails. Stretch the neck and chop off the head. This keeps your fingers away from the descending axe blade. You will likely get sprayed with blood as the chicken's heart pumps the blood out. The chicken will not be feeling any pain since pain is felt in the brain and the head is off.

2. There is a technique that involves sticking a narrow sharp knife blade up through the roof of the mouth into the brain, killing the bird instantly. I am not crazy about this method since the bird is not bled out very much–but it does keep the blood off your clothes. This is the method used by some commercial packing houses. You can, of course, cut the bird's throat or cut its head off to bleed it out after it has stopped the involuntary jerking and kicking. This is a good method to use with turkeys, ducks and geese.

3. One method that was preferred by my parents was a technique for dislocating the bird's neck and breaking the spinal cord. You hold the bird's legs firmly between the fingers of one hand, place the top of the bird's head in the palm of your other hand with the bird's neck between the first two fingers, and while pulling, bend the bird's head back against its neck. As the neck bones separated you bring your fingers together to crush the spinal cord. It sounds a bit clumsy, but it a clean and efficient way to kill the bird without getting any blood on yourself. Then, as above, you bleed the bird out after it has stopped kicking. With very young chickens too much pull will pull the bird's head off.

4. One method I have never used is to take the bird by it's head and swing it around until the head comes off–a crude method with no class.

5. Animal feed supply stores (in the country) sell a killing funnel.

You put the bird head down into the funnel with its head sticking out of the small end and then either cut its throat or cut its head right off. The main advantage to this method is the bird does not thrash round spraying blood while it is bleeding out. It also eliminates one problem—sometimes a freshly killed bird will thrash around so much that it bruises the meat and breaks bones (especially the wing bones). Since the wings are held in by the funnel no damage occurs to the bones or meat. This is the method that I prefer.

Plucking the feathers: Chickens *can* be dry plucked, but it does a poor job. To remove all the feathers, including the pin feathers, it is necessary to immerse the entire bird in hot water for enough time to loosen the feathers. Heat a large can of water to a hot, but not boiling temperature. For more than one bird we use a metal trash can balanced on two cement blocks and light a wood fire underneath. The time of immersion is proportional to the heat of the water. Bring the water up to, say, 140°F, dip the chicken in and move it around to get water to the base of the feathers for a few seconds and try pulling a few feathers. If they are hard to pull out then re-immerse the bird for a few more seconds. If the feathers come out too easily the water was too hot or the bird was in too long and you have probably started to cook the skin. It takes a little practice to be able to judge the correct times of immersion as the temperature of the water rises or cools. Having loosened the feathers in the hot water, hang the bird up by its feet with two pieces of string from the rafters (in the barn?) so that its legs are pulled apart and pluck out all the feathers. It should be about five feet off the ground. On older birds you may have to use a pair of pliers to pull out the wing feathers. It does not matter if the water gets a little grungy as you will be washing the bird clean as a last thing before wrapping it. For turkeys you definitely need at least a thirty gallon metal trash can and a pair of pliers.

Dressing out the plucked chicken: Leave the legs on until you have finished everything else, they give you something to hold on to, then remove them at the joint where the scaly skin on the legs starts.

With the bird on a cutting board, make a small cut (just barely big enough to squeeze your hand in) across the bird's body at the lower rear of the body between the last bones of the rib cage and the tail. Reach in and pull everything out. Scrape the inside clean with your fingers being sure to get the lungs out of the cavities in which they sit in between the ribs. Go to the front of the bird and cut off the neck at the body. Put your hand into the neck cavity and pull everything out—the craw is very well attached and a little hard to get started out. You should be able to put your hand up the rear and touch your hand in the front. Depending on your tastes, some of the items you have removed are very edible when cooked and used in gravies etc. Save the heart, the liver, the neck you removed. Some people even use the gizzard with the tough membrane removed. Now wash the bird inside and out very thoroughly in clean water and pat dry. This is the time to decide if you want it whole or cut up. Wrap it, or the pieces of it, in freezer paper, mark the outside with the contents and the date and put it in the freezer—or take it to the stove and start cooking!

Turkeys, ducks, and geese: There is no difference in the raising of the chicks and very little difference in the feed. Geese will eat some grass and have been used in the past to weed out grass in strawberry patches. Geese also make outstanding watch dogs and will raise a great noisy fuss if any strange person or animal approaches.

The ducks and geese, of course, would benefit from access to a body of water.

Turkeys are a little more difficult and delicate to raise. They are perhaps the stupidest of birds. If they get frightened they will pile up in a corner and suffocate the lower ones. If it rains the young turkey poults (chicks) will tilt their heads up and drown in the rain. They must NEVER be raised on a surface that has been used for chickens in the previous three years. There is a disease called "blackhead" that is carried by chickens without any noticeable effect that can be transmitted to turkeys and it is fatal to the turkeys. Turkeys benefit enormously from being raised on alfalfa—it cuts the feed costs down quite a bit and makes a significant improvement in the taste. Turkeys raised on organic feed (no anti-biotics) and on alfalfa pasture (or throw some fresh cut alfalfa in daily) are really better tasting than you can imagine.

Due to the increased difficulty with raising turkeys (and it is not, in fact, really very much more difficult) there is a much better profit in turkeys, particularly if sold locally as organically raised. You can take orders from your neighbors sell them at the size the customers wants—anywhere for about eight pounds on up to thirty or more pounds. There is much more profit in the birds sold at lighter weights since the conversion ratio of feed to meat declines as the birds get older.

CHAPTER TWELVE

SWINE

Traditionally it was the pigs that paid the mortgage on the farm. Pigs are a much maligned animal–they do not smell any worse than any other animal–if they are kept clean. Any animal that is kept in filthy conditions will smell, and pigs are no exception. It is critical to know that clean conditions, good food and plentiful water are essential to the health of any animal and make a significant difference in their profitability. So on to the small farmer's friend–the pig.

Nomenclature: Baby pigs that are still nursing, or just weaned, are called "weaners". Female maiden pigs are called gilts. Female pigs that are bred or have had young are called sows. Male pigs are boars. Castrated male pigs are barrows.

Buying pigs: Pigs are normally only sold at three stages of their lives: Full size and ready to butcher; breeding sows and boars; and just weaned piglets. We are interested only in weaned piglets— and maybe in boars if we get deeply into raising pigs. We can raise our own sows.

Piglets can be weaned off the sow at any age from 3 weeks old up to eight or nine weeks. The normal age for weaning is either six weeks or eight weeks. For our purpose we want piglets that have been nursing on the sow as long as possible–and eight weeks is ideal.

What are we looking for in a young pig–a "weaner"? Of course its health is the primary consideration.

Healthy young weaners will exhibit the following characteristics:

Bright lively looking eyes–a look of intelligence in the eyes (pigs are more intelligent than dogs).

No sign of any skin problems. The skin is firm with perhaps only a very slight dandruff-like powder in the hair. The hair is not long and coarse–that is the sign of a runt pig. There should be no sign of any cracking or broken blood vessels on the skin–these are signs of erysipelas. I prefer the white breeds of pigs since this makes for cleaner appearing hams, but this is a personal preference. Some breeds exhibit a wide range of coloring.

A quite long and straight snout is preferred. It is essential that the snout does not have any inclination to the side as this is a sign of rhinitis–a degenerative disease that rots the nose away. I like the nose long because it just seems that they eat better and stay healthier–and it easier to tell if they have the rhinitis.

The ears should be quite opaque and not appear to be a little transparent. The ears may be erect or droopy depending on the breed. Good ears are an indication that there is no iron deficiency. If they are otherwise healthy, iron deficiency can be quite easily corrected–I'll get into that a little when we look at raising our own weaners.

Healthy piglets are active! They squeal and run around. The tails curl tight against the rear and they can run–you don't appreciate just how fast they are until you try to catch one. When observed from a distance they appear playful with each other. When buying less than the full litter the ones that you want are the ones that are the biggest and are the hardest catch–ideally 30 to 35 pounds in weight.

Many years ago, before the advent of vegetable cooking oils, there were breeds of pigs specifically raised for making lard–fat pigs–very, very fat pigs!–in old illustrations some look like fifty-five gallon drums with short legs. In some backwoods areas there is still some of that lard strain of breeding in the pigs–we don't want it. Look at the general overall shape of the piglets. We want a long lean pig with a straight back and evidence of good size hams. Fat pigs make fatty bacon, fatty hams, fatty pork chops, etc.

Castration: If raised for butchering, male pigs (boars) must be castrated. If they are not castrated they bring several problems. If they are housed with their female litter mates they will breed them at too early an age. Boars will fight with each other. Boar meat is not fit to eat, having too strong a taste. And boars, as they get older, get bad tempered and dangerous.

Weaner boars can be castrated as young as three weeks of age, though I prefer about six to eight weeks, while still nursing on the sow. There is really only one successful way of castrating a boar and that is surgically–the use of Burdizo pliers and rubber bands is not very successful with pigs. I will not go into the actual techniques for castrating in this book. It is quite easy to do and quite safe for the pig. I have castrated 500 or more piglets without ever losing one. When done at a very early age, it seems that they almost don't notice it–a couple of squeals and they go back to feeding. Some people like the by-product of castration, the "mountain oysters"–I always toss them to the dog–he likes a treat once in a while too. Get your veterinarian (not an amateur neighbor) to show you the correct way to do it.

If you think that you might possibly keep one or more of the weaners as breeding sows, then buy all female weaners–it will give you more choice when you get them up to a decent enough size to be able to select the one(s) to keep.

When you get them home: Have a clean pen ready with feed and water available. Sprinkle just a little iron powder (from the feed store) on the dry feed, or put liquid iron in the water–follow the recommendations on the package or bottle.

Now, and this can save you a lot of work, stand by the pen and wait until one of the weaners defecates. Immediately pick up the feces with a shovel and put it where you want them to deposit all the manure. Do this two or three times until you see them start to use the area you have selected. From now on they will deposit all the manure in that same spot and you can clean them out with just a quick shovel or two every day. The pen will stay clean and the bedding area (liberally supplied with clean straw) will stay

clean for weeks at a time. Replenish the bedding straw as needed–
they will eat a little of it. Incidentally this regimen works just as
well if you bring older sows and boars home–they too are smart
enough to keep clean if you will let them.

Worming pigs: All bought pigs should be wormed immediately
on arrival at home before mixing them with any other pigs. There
are few pigs that do not have at least one of the ascarids
(roundworms, pinworms, threadworms). Worming medicines are
usually added to drinking water. Use a lot of care, worming
medicines are poison and should be dispensed *exactly* as prescribed
in the label instructions. Keep these, and any other medications,
well out of the reach of children and pets.

Feeding and care in general: Pigs are omnivorous–they will eat
anything that you can eat–and enjoy it just as much as you do.

Commercial pig feeds come in a variety of protein and mineral
levels. Most feeds also come in either a ground or a pelleted form–
the pelleted form seems to be the most palatable and there is less
waste:

1. Starter feed for young pigs–a high protein feed designed to give
   them a good start.
2. Grower–for growing pigs (duh!). A medium protein level feed.
3. Finisher is for putting the final finish on market hogs. A lower
   protein level designed to put meat on while not adding fat.
4. Sow feed is specially formulated to provide the sow with the
   nourishment she needs to feed herself and the nursing piglets.
5. Bran is only for certain specialized uses.

There are two basic types of hog feeders. One type is the *metal
self feeder* sold in feed stores. They are good, but a little expensive.
If you study the dimensions of one in the store, particularly the
sizes of the opening at the bottom, you can make one out of wood
that will work just as well and cost a whole lot less. Pigs are smart
enough not to overeat if there is food available 24 hours a day. If it
is the right feed for their age they will thrive, grow and stay healthy
on a self feed diet.

You can make *metal trough feeders* out of the inside of an old hot water heater. Cut a nine inch wide opening in one lengthwise and weld a couple of eighteen inch long pieces of old car springs across the bottom to stop it rolling over. It is smart to also put several of straps across the top to stop them from lying in it.

I do not recommend feeding restaurant waste to pigs–I have lost pigs due to them ingesting fiberglass cigarette butts in restaurant waste. I suppose that in California, where there is no smoking in restaurants (lucky people!), the waste may be OK to use, but it is a nasty smelly business that takes any pleasure out of raising nice healthy pigs.

All animals need *water* to be available all the time. If you use a metal trough for watering, the pigs will try to get in it to take a bath if there are no straps across the top to stop them. There are *automatic waterers* that, when attached to a wall and connected to a water supply, put fresh water in the fixture any time it is used. The pig has to push a valve thing with its nose and water comes out. Pigs are smart and they learn to do this very quickly–however, note that baby pigs cannot work these devices until eight or ten weeks old.

Almost any absorbent material can be used for bedding, but straw from any grain crop (except some barleys) is the preferred bedding. It absorbs any moisture, it is non-toxic if eaten, and it makes a significant contribution to the quality of the manure when it goes on the garden–be generous, that cement floor is a cold place to lie on at night! If you fasten a two by six on edge across the middle of the floor of the pen and put the bedding straw on one side, the pigs will keep that side clean.

Litters can be mixed once they are weaned–I do not recommend having more than about 50 growing pigs in one (large) pen. They should all be about the same age and size.

There are standard markings for identifying individual pigs that involve ear notching and/or tattooing, however the small farmer always knows each pig by name.

A last comment on care of all pigs–pigs can sunburn, particularly the white breeds. And pigs cannot sweat–that is why they like to roll in mud in hot weather to cool themselves off. Their skin dries out in the sun and wind. If they do not have access to a place to roll in *clean* mud, then they will benefit from a little (non-detergent) motor oil dribbled on their backs once in a while to replace the natural oils they are losing–use new oil, not nasty dirty old stuff.

Feeding growing pigs: Pigs are very healthy animals. Given half a chance they will thrive on any reasonably sensible diet–remember pigs, like people are omnivorous–this means that besides fruit and vegetables they will eat meat—don't let little children EVER get in a pen with any pig–pigs are not fussy what kind of meat they eat. Like pigs bought at auctions or privately, weaners should be wormed a week or two after they are weaned–see "Worming pigs" above.

There is a simple standard feeding schedule for raising good quality pork and ham without excessive fat. And the first thing to note is that is does NOT include corn! I learned to raise pigs in Canada where the Canadian government pays a premium on top of the market price for each pig that grades out at a quality suitable for export as Canadian bacon. The standards are very rigid to get this extra bonus. It is a simple fact that corn fed hogs would never get that bonus. The bacon in our American stores is a disgrace. The fat content is indicative of a striving for weight and not for quality. If that is the quality of bacon and pork that you want, then read no further–just feed corn and enjoy the fat that you raise.

Quality pork is raised on oats and barley, with some mineral supplements. It takes about 700 pounds of feed to raise the kind of bacon that we want. 100 pounds of starter, 500 pounds of grower and 100 pounds of finisher. When buying commercial feed, look at the label for the ingredients. The chances are you will not find one without some corn, but hopefully there will not be too much. A 30-35 pound weaner raised on this diet, with adequate water and clean surroundings will weigh right about at 205 to 215 pounds at 5 to 5½ months of age. The barrows will be at the 215 and the gilts will be at the 205. They will dress out to 160 to 165 pounds of high quality, low fat meat.

If you are not sure you can judge their weights, there is a little trick you can practice. As the pigs grow, let them get familiar with you, scratch behind the ears and never hit them. Carry a dressmaker's cloth tape measure and get them used to you measuring them around the chest just back of the front legs when they are eating–it is not hard to get their confidence when they are not being abused. They will weigh the desired weight when they measure just about exactly 42 inches around the chest–trust me! Most American hog producers take their pigs up to 250 or more pounds–that extra 40 pounds is all lard—from the corn.

Breeding sows: Your best source of sows is the pigs you have raised yourself. Buying a sow from someone else really is "buying a pig in poke"–you don't know just why it is being sold. It may be barren, only have very small litters, be addicted to eating its own young, or who knows what else could be wrong with it.

A good time to pick out the gilts to keep as sows is right at the time they are ready to butcher–205-215 pounds and five to six months old. They could be picked out a little younger, 180 or so pounds and bred then. That is the age and size used by commercial pig factories, but I think they are a little too small when they farrow (give birth) to be good milking mothers. Pick gilts from big litters. Be very selective. Pick out the long lean pigs–they make the best bacon. Pick out the biggest–they will have the biggest babies. Count the number of teats that look functional–there should be at least 12 working teats if the sow is going to be able to feed a decent size litter. Pay a little attention to the gilt's personality–she will be bigger and heavier than you are and has sharper teeth–you want to be able to get in the pen and help with the farrowing without her getting upset or attacking you. Look them over very critically– they represent a half of the genes going into the next generation, and they are the difference between successful pig raising and a losing hobby.

You can tell when a gilt or a sow is in heat and willing to be bred by the appearance of the vulva–it becomes fuller, softer looking and redder, almost inflamed. She will arch her back and squeal a little when you scratch it, indicating a willingness to be bred. A sow will come into heat a few days after farrowing–a bad time to breed her–it is hard on a sow to be pregnant while still milking. A good heavy milking sow actually gives more milk than some cows! She will also come into heat about three to five days after her babies are weaned off her, and this is a good time to breed her. This lets you get two litters a year from each sow. Commercial producers push their sows to five litters every two years by weaning the piglets too young and breeding the sow while still nursing the piglets–false economy for the small farmer.

It is normally better to take the sow to the boar. Sometimes if you bring the boar to the sow she will attack it quite viciously for invading her space. Some think that two breedings a day apart give a bigger litter. If you own the boar and it is easy and handy to do so, then why not?

The gestation period for a pig is 114 days (three months, three weeks, and three days). This is quite firm and only varies by one or two days.

Care of bred and nursing sows: While a bred sow will belly out in her pregnancy, do not let her get too fat. It is a problem with sows and boars that they do not seem to ever stop growing until they die of old age. That nice looking 200 pound gilt is going to end up being a 600 pound sow after a couple of years have passed. This tendency to keep growing presents us with a couple of problems. One is finding a suitable size boar that can breed our 200 pound gilt and at the other extreme finding a boar to breed our 600 pound sow. During her pregnancy feed her sow ration and if she is over eating and gaining too much weight cut her feed back to a measured amount. Give your food scraps to the pregnant sow in preference to any other pigs–the variety is good for them and hand feeding them helps them to regard you as a friend and not a jailer. One thing to be careful of is that a very thin sow may turn on her young and eat them, if she is hungry enough. A second problem is that when sows get larger they get clumsy and can, and will, roll on top of the little pigs and crush or suffocate them.

About two days before she is due to farrow change her diet to a wet mash of bran. This helps prevent constipation which can cause problems during the delivery.

Wean the pigs away by taking them away for one night, let them nurse the next morning then never again. The sow will get excited, but gets over it–at this time be careful as she can get very mean.

Housing for sows and their litters: A good farrowing pen takes a little more work than a regular pig pen. Mount a two by four rail or a metal rail all around the pen about five inches above the floor and five inches out from the wall. This is to prevent that clumsy sow from crushing the babies against the wall when she lies down or rolls over.

Fence off a triangular piece in one corner for the piglets to sleep in. This should be about four feet by four feet off the corner with a five inch high access for the baby piglets to get under to get away from the sow. Over this triangle hang a heat lamp to keep the babies warm. You want about 85-90°F at the height of the piglets' back for the first week or so. It helps to have this fenced off corner next to the aisle where you can just reach in to get a piglet without going into the pen–it is less disturbing for the sow.

Housing for all pigs: Pigs benefit from dry housing and also from some fresh air. But be aware that unless you have put hog rings in their noses they will uproot anything and everything that is not thick concrete. If there are holes or cracks in a concrete floor the pigs will work on it until they can heave up the concrete. Pigs have powerful shoulder muscles and noses–a 250 pound sow can lift up the side of a car with her nose. In an inside pen pigs need about 50 square feet of floor space each. A sow with a litter needs about 75 square feet.

As an alternative to barn housing with a concrete floor there is a practice that is very effective for the small farm/large garden. You can build a small hog house out of about three sheets of plywood (at least ½ inch thick) in an "A" shape configuration. Use two sheets for the walls and one for one end. Make it quite strong. It will be about eight feet long and four feet wide at the bottom. There is no floor. Close one end and open the other end into an attached four foot wide by eight foot long wire pen three foot high built on a two by four frame. This structure, with handles attached is light enough for two people to lift/drag the whole thing a few feet every few days. We put one of these in our garden and my wife and I moved it as it was needed—every three or four days. Each time we moved it we moved it so the inside area was on new clean, dry ground. Throw a couple of slices of straw in the house for bedding. The pigs rooted up all their old bedding out in the wire run and anything and every thing that had been left in the ground from the previous growing season. After moving it I immediately turned over the run area with a garden fork to incorporate the manure. This system is almost completely free of flies and smell and does fantastic things to the garden soil. This is a good size for up to three pigs.

Care of newborn piglets: Important!–you can save at least one piglet, and maybe more by being present during the birth of the litter. A sow's litter will vary from one (or none) to up to a normal maximum of sixteen. Baby pigs are born almost blind and weighing about 3 to 3½ pounds (if you have been feeding the sow properly).

As mentioned above, have a heat lamp over the fenced off corner so you can put the babies in the warm area as they are born.

The sequence of events as baby piglets are born is quite interesting to observe. As each baby is born just about blind it will stumble around and will automatically head for the sow's head. She will bite off the umbilical cord and the baby will turn around and head for the sow's teats to feed. Let it feed for a few minutes or until it quits, then put it under the heat lamp. This is one point where you can save it's life–sometimes the sow, while in the throes of labor, will jerk her legs around and kick the baby off course, the baby will head off into the distance and never find its way back without your help.

As you put each baby under the heat there are a couple of things you can do for it. Using a small pair of side cutting pliers, clip just the points off the four needle teeth–these are very sharp little (usually) black teeth. These teeth can scratch the sow's udder causing her to reject the babies or to get infections on the udder.

Give the baby a dose of iron (follow the package directions very carefully). Pigs are born anemic and the sow's milk is deficient in iron. On larger farms this iron is given in the form of an injection into the hip.

If the sow hasn't done a good job on the umbilical cord, clip it with a pair of scissors to about one and a half inches long–dip the end of the cord in a small container of weak iodine to prevent umbilical infections. At about the time the afterbirth comes, put a dab of iodine on the sow's nose to prevent her from rejecting the piglets due to their smell.

In the wild, sows eat the afterbirth but for us this can cause problems. Once in a while the sow will like the taste of blood and turn to eating the babies–so if you have the chance pick the afterbirth up on a shovel and get it out of the pen. Do not let her have access to any piglets born dead.

Out of each litter there will usually be two runts. (See "Healthy young weaners" above for identifying runts). One will be distinctly smaller than the others and one will be only slightly smaller. The runts are the two end ones on the umbilical cord while still in the sow–they get less nutrition through the sow's blood flow in the umbilical cord. If there is a large litter, say over 12, it is best to dispose of the smaller runt–it is not going to be able to fight it's way to a nipple on the udder against its bigger siblings. The larger runt makes a good whole roasted pig when it reaches about 50 to 80 pounds–it will probably never catch up to the others–have a barbecue with whole spit roasted pig and invite all the family and neighbors! During the eight weeks of nursing it will be time to castrate the boars (see castration above)–this is one good reason to have the baby area easily accessible.

At about 3 or 4 weeks of age start putting a little pig starter loose on the floor in the corner bedroom. As they eat it, put more in every day in a container. They will continue to nurse but will benefit from the vitamins and minerals in the starter and have no setback or problems continuing to eat and grow when they are weaned.

Boars: Boars are a pain in the neck. They are non-productive except for about 5 minutes once in a while. They get big and dangerous. There is no demand for boar meat. Castrating a 600 pound boar is an exercise that provides lots of excitement and adrenalin production–it involves a 55 gallon drum and a couple of strong men. Even after castration, boar meat only brings about 3 cents a pound as animal feed. There are methods for removing a boar's tusks that involve some slightly hazardous work with a crow-bar and hammer that I am not going to even try and cover. If you are lucky, one of your neighbors will keep a boar that you can use.

The rapid growth and short gestation of pigs presents a prob-lem in that you can get a nice young boar and use him on your sows. About 8 months later you have a new batch of gilts that you do not want to breed back to their father and maybe a new boar that you do not want to use on his mother or sisters–so you have to sell the older boar and the new boar or buy new sows or gilts. Then buy a new boar. Or find someone with whom to trade boars. Most commercial hog farmers will not let you have use of their boars on your gilts or sows because they are afraid of bringing in disease, however they will sell you a young weaner boar that is unrelated to your stock or sell you a boar that they cannot use any more. In any case, you will not get any profit or good meat from a boar.

Growing your own feed: It's possible, but realistically only on a large scale. It is impractical to try to grow, harvest and grind up an appropriate mixture of oats, barley, or other grains to feed to your pigs. Concentrate your efforts on growing food for your own table or for sale and buy commercial pig feed. This being said, I must point out that there is very little *cash* profit in raising any livestock on store bought feed. Using the "A" frame housing method that I outlined in "Housing for all pigs" above, we found that if we raise three pigs in that portable housing and sold two we would get 160 pounds of pork, ham and sausages almost, but not quite, free.

Fencing: There are only two types of fences that will reliably keep pigs confined. The best is the specially made hog fencing that is so much stronger than regular fencing. The other is electric fence–the hogs will try it and learn to respect it—but they will try it every day to make sure it is still working. It is very disturbing to get a call at 5 am from a neighbor complaining that twenty or so of your pigs are in his flower beds—it makes for bad neighbors.

Butchering your hogs: You can do it yourself. In the back woods of the south many hogs are butchered and the hams smoked at home. It is a messy business best done on a crispy cold fall morning when there are no flies around. There are government pamphlets that detail how to cut up a pig and how to smoke the hams, season the sausages, etc. Or get a knowledgeable neighbor to teach you. I have done it and I hated doing it–those pigs were my friends just as much as my dog is! I prefer to deliver my pigs to a professional slaughter house and pay them to return to me a box of nicely packaged meat.

CHAPTER THIRTEEN

CATTLE

Nomenclature: Male cattle are bulls. Castrated males are steers–when they have been trained to work in harness they are called oxen. Young of both sexes are calves. A female calf is a heifer. A heifer that has had a calf is a cow.

General: Cattle are quite expensive to get into and the return can be quite slow compared for example to chickens or pigs. On the other hand they do not mature all of a sudden and have to be disposed off at bargain prices, they can be held for many months waiting for a better price–if your pocket can stand the wait.

You need room to keep cattle. In the west, up to 40 acres per cow, and sometimes more. In the eastern and southern states a good pasture will support cattle at about one to two acres per cow, plus more for winter-time hay. If you have to buy hay you will certainly lose money on cattle–the profit margin is not enough to support buying feed.

Breeds: There are two basic breeds of cattle: Beef cattle and milk cattle. Their body types and milk production are quite distinctly different.

The milk cow. The popular conception of a cow is the Holstein (Holstein-Friesian)–a quite large, bony, black and white animal. Holsteins originally came from Holland and northern Germany. Holsteins are the milk producers of the modern world giving enormous amounts of milk–many gallons more than any calf could use. The milk produced by the Holstein is quite low in butter fat compared to some other breeds. Holstein steers have been used as oxen since they are a large strong animal. Another common breed is the Jersey. Jerseys (from the Jersey Islands) are a smaller animal, usually brown in color that have a lower volume of production of milk but a very high butter fat content when compared to the milk of a Holstein. There are other breeds that are less common but popular with some farmers, such breeds as the Guernsey for example. One warning: ALL the bulls of the milk breeds are un-predictable and dangerous—never, ever, trust a bull of Holstein or Jersey breeding, even if you have raised it from a baby—one day it will turn on you.

The beef cow of today is the Hereford. Herefords originally came from the shire of Hereford in England. They are a blocky, heavy, red (often with a white face) animal. Hereford cows, and indeed all the other beef breeds, give just enough milk to raise fine big calves. Herefords have been cross bred with a variety of other animals, specially in the Southwest where a tolerance of the hot summers and scanty feed are necessary. They have been crossed with such breeds as Brahmas, Longhorns, etc.

In days past *multi-purpose cattle* were common. The Brown Swiss, for example, is a pretty good milk cow, gives a good quantity of beef, and the steers are good strong oxen.

Buying cattle in general: Cows, calves, bulls and steers can be bought at all ages. They are sold privately and at auctions, both at farm auctions and at auction barns. Sales at farms that are going out of business for one reason or another are a good place to find decent animals—if the whole herd is being sold then you need not be afraid that you are getting a cull.

Take someone with you who knows cattle—they are quite an expensive investment and it easy to get stuck with a barren cow, one with a non-functioning teat, a calf with bad scours (an intestinal problem that kills) or some other problem or disease.

Buying calves: Most calves that are sold at very young ages are from the milk breeds or cross breeds. The majority are bull calves from milk herds. You can expect to pay quite high prices for fe-male calves of any breed and for any calves of the beef breeds.

Many calves are sold as "day olds"–although they may be several days old. Strangely enough a calf that really is just one day old is a better buy than one that is several days old. This is because many milk farmers take new born bull calves away from the cow (they don't ever let the cow get used to having its calf nursing on it) and they put the calf in a pen in the corner with other bull baby calves. These calves will be trucked to a local auction yard once a week to be sold–a milk farmer has a use for only one bull. So, some of the calves they take to the sale may be up to one week old–and have never been fed or watered. By that time they are sick—very sick. They get a disease called "scours". When a calf is scouring it has a very liquid diarrhea that smells quite bad. If the scours progresses enough it strips the lining out of the calf's intestine to the point where the calf cannot be saved.

Look at the calf's eyes, they should be bright and alert. Its nose should be moist and not dried up. Its nose should not be running. Being frisky is not a real good indicator since some sick calves are quite frisky for a while. Check its back legs for diarrhea– this can be tricky to analyze visually since even healthy calves normally have very loose yellow stools–but the smell is distinctly different for a scouring calf. A calf that is standing with its back humped up and looks sick, is sick–when it is obviously sick it is too late to save it.

Raising calves: A calf with a mild case of scours is quite treatable– and make no mistake, any calf that you buy from an auction yard will have the start of scours, it is a highly contagious bacterial disease of calves that is endemic to all auction yards. You must treat any day old calf that you acquire from anywhere as having scours. The treatment will not harm a healthy calf. The treatment can be in the form of an injection or by an addition to the milk in a bottle fed calf. Talk to you veterinarian *before* you buy any calves– get him to provide you with the medication that you need. The best time to treat a calf is right now! In the loading area of the auction yard if you can, before you even load it in your truck. Newly bought calves must be kept segregated from other calves until the scour treatment is successful due to the contagious nature of the disease.

Day old calves can be bottle fed quite successfully nowadays. You can feed milk from a cow or milk made from powder. The Purina Company makes an excellent milk substitute for bottle feeding–it comes in twenty-five pound bags. Calf feeding bottles are one quart size–although at first the calf won't drink a full quart. The technique for getting them to suck on a bottle is quite simple. You put some milk on your fingers and let the calf suck it off. As you do this you gradually introduce the nipple of the bottle into its mouth along with your fingers. One thing to note–the natural position for a calf when it is nursing on a cow is with its neck and shoulders low and its head pointed up into the air to get to the udder. In that position they can swallow without any trouble. You must simulate this position for the calves and point the nipple almost straight down when you are bottle feeding them in order to avoid the possibility of getting milk into their lungs.

Forty-five years ago when I first started farming you would consider yourself lucky if you could raise even a half of the calves that you brought home. The survival rate for day old calves not nursing on their mothers was so poor that you could buy a nice day old bull calf for less than two dollars. Nowadays calves are much more expensive but the medications to treat them are very good. Although I do not like to keep any livestock on anti-biotic or any other medication, it does seem to be necessary in the case of bottle fed calves. Fortunately the medications are long gone from their systems by the time we start milking them or eating them.

Sometimes a calf may be sick enough that it can no longer suck on a bottle. While you are talking to your vet about medications for scours, ask him (or her) about tube feeding day old calves. He will supply or recommend the proper size tubing to do this quite simple thing and show you how to do it without getting the tube into the calf's lungs. A calf that is successfully tube fed two or three times can usually be saved. The special milk mixture fed to sick calves has medication to treat the damage to the intestine–if the intestine is not too badly damaged.

Initially you must warm the milk to body temperature for newborn calves, but as they get a week or two older you can reduce the temperature and even end up just taking it out of the refrigerator. Once a calf is eating properly they have an almost insatiable appetite for more and more milk or powdered milk substitute. At about a month of age introduce them to calf feed in a pelleted form. At first they will eat very little, but once they get a taste over several weeks for the molasses that is quite often an ingredient they will eat enough that you can start to think about weaning them. Given the opportunity, they will never wean themselves and will take milk for as long as you are willing to give it to them. We only give in to their craving if we are wanting to raise them for veal or baby beef. At the same time you introduduce the calf pellets give them access to some *high* quality hay, preferably nice *leafy* (not stalky) alfalfa. Change the hay often even daily (give what you remove to one of the older cows) and keep nice clean fresh hay in front of the calves.

Castrating: Castration of bull calves is best done at a very early age–a few weeks old is best.

Why castrate? Bulls are hard to handle and dangerous. Many people don't like the taste of bull meat. Steers seem to grow faster than bulls. Only the bull of your choice gets to breed your cows and heifers—steers do not bother your cows and heifers by trying to breed them. Steers are the only animals strong enough and docile enough to be used in harness as oxen.

There are several ways of castrating a bull.

Surgically—by removing the testicles. The advantages: Guaranteed no failures–they have no testicles to regenerate as can happen with other methods. Disadvantages: This is surgery with its possible attendant complications (infection, possible blood loss, etc.)

With Burdizo pliers–special very heavy (and expensive) pliers that crush the cord to the testicles without breaking the skin. The testicles wither away for lack of a blood supply. Advantages: No problems with infections from surgery and no problems with getting fly blown. Disadvantages: Once in a while the cord is not properly crushed and the bull remains functionally fertile.

Rubber bands–these are not your regular office rubber bands but rather specially made, very strong bands that have a very small hole in the center. They are applied with special pliers that stretch them enough to slip over the scrotum. The rubber band constricts the scrotum, cutting off the blood supply and the scrotum eventually falls off. Advantages: The special pliers are a lot cheaper to buy and the rubber bands are very cheap. No problems with infections from surgery and no problems with getting fly blown. Disadvantages: Once in a while the rubber band breaks and the bull remains functionally fertile.

My recommendation: Rubber bands. You can check for the withering of the testicles with your hand after a week or so to be sure it is taking place or if the scrotum has fallen off. You can always use another rubber band if necessary. Note that rubber bands come in several sizes–read the package carefully to get the right size. One caution–do not ever put one of your fingers inside the hole in the rubber band. If it slips off the pliers and closes on your finger you must very quickly cut the band with something very sharp, like a razor blade, even if you have to cut your finger doing it or you risk serious damage to your finger.

Dehorning: Some breeds have been bred to be polled (hornless). Horns on cattle of all ages and sexes are a danger to you and to each other. The only cattle that should keep their horns are oxen.

There are several ways of removing the horns:

Caustic paste: You can apply a caustic paste (bought at a feed store) to the horn buds of calves. It burns. The calves do not like it and it will scar you if you get it on yourself. Not recommended.

Hacksaw or other saw: This works fine on the first horn until you hit the big nerve in the center of the horn, and then look out! Blood sprays everywhere and that cow will explode into action!

Special de-horning tool: Looks like a pair of bolt cutters. It works just fine if the animal well secured. Again the first horn is easy, it is the second one that is the problem–the cow no longer trusts you– with good reason.

Rubber bands: See "Rubber bands" above in the castration paragraphs. This is perhaps the most humane way since there is no immediate stabbing pain for the animal. That super strong rubber band gradually squeezes itself into the horn until, one day, the cow rubs its horn against a tree or fence post and the horn snaps off. Again, make sure you have the right rubber bands for the job.

Calving: If you have treated your heifers and cows with some care and not abused them you will have no trouble assisting them to have their calves and milking them after. Get your animals used be being handled right from being young calves. Particularly for animals you intend to milk you should teach them to be halter trained and to be led around. A skittish young heifer having her first calf will not let you assist if she doesn't trust you–and they quite often do need a little help, especially with their first calf.

Ideally a cow or heifer should have her calf out in a nice clean grassy field in an area where she can be alone to have her calf with nothing bothering her–but where you can find her easily. Don't let her go off into deep brush or forest in case she needs help. A small private paddock near the house is ideal.

Problems in calving do not happen all that often. Cows are big animals and the act of giving birth comes quite easily to them in most cases. Normally a calf is born head first with its two front feet each side of its head. The most common problem a cow can have is a breech birth–call a vet immediately if you see the back legs start to come out first. Take a moment to study a cow or a calf's front and back feet and observe the difference so you can identity them if necessary. If the cow has been in labor more than six or eight hours she needs expert help. Even if a cow should lose her calf, she can still be milked.

If you don't want to milk the cow and want her to nurse her calf you can have another day old calf handy and, as the calf is born, smear some of the wet coating from the new born calf on to the one standing by. Then let the cow lick them both clean—she can't tell whether she has had one calf or had twins and she will care for them both. Nature will ensure that she has enough milk for both of them. Some Holstein cows have been known to feed up to four calves this way!

Milk Cows and Milking:

You don't need a pedigree Holstein-Friesen cow to provide all the milk you need for your house, its calf and maybe milk left over to make into cheese and butter. Almost any grade cow will do that–and her calf will make another heifer or a beef steer.

Buying a milk cow: Professional milk producers grow obsessive about what they call "suspension". They are referring to the muscles and construction of the parts of the rear of the cow that keep the udder up in the air. Very heavy producing Holstein cows get to have very big udders–big enough for them to step on their teats with their own hoofs and damage the teat. While we are not really interested in cows with championship levels of production, we also don't want our cows stepping on their own teats. Look for a firm tight udder, big but held up close to the body. If you get a chance compare the rear end of an older milk cow with a young one and see how the muscles between the back legs have stretched.

We want our milk cow to have four functioning teats. There is a disease called mastitis that can cause a teat to become non-functional. A cow's udder has four quarters with one teat to a quarter. If one teat doesn't work then the quarter won't produce, or will get inflamed and eventually cause major problems. Early stages of mastitis can be treated with injections of anti-biotics directly into the quarter–but chances are once a cow gets mastitis it will keep recurring. If the cow is actually milking at the time you buy it be sure to try out each teat. If there is no sign of milk in one of the teats or if the cow flinches or kicks out there are problems that you don't want to take home.

For all cows, examine the animal with great care. Study its feet and see if it limps at all. Examine its eyes for signs of infection or blindness. Mucus running out of its nose can be bad–though we all get colds once in a while. It should be fairly alert–cows are naturally phlegmatic animals and not that lively even when healthy. If you have doubts about your ability to pick out healthy animals, take a knowledgeable friend along with you–but use your own judgment as well.

Commercial dairies keep their best cows for several years, letting them have as many as fifteen calves over that period. At some point they sell off the older cows. This could be your chance to get a high quality pedigree cow at a cheap price that can give just one more calf. If that calf is a heifer then you have gotten yourself a future prime milk cow. That old cow will still make hundreds of pounds of hamburger even if the steaks are tough and she will give you lots of milk for up to a year before that.

Milking cows: Cows are usually milked in a stanchion. A stanchion is piece of equipment that opens up to let the cow have access to a tray of grain or a manger of hay. The stanchion closes around its neck to hold it in place while it is being milked.

Cows being milked by hand are always milked from the right side of the cow–with one exception–that is my wife who insists on milking from the left side for no known reason. The cows can get used to it if they have to. Milking by hand is a simple skill that develops very strong hands for the milker.

Here is the step by step sequence for hand milking:
1. Put the cow in the stanchion. If you have gotten her used to eating through the stanchion before she freshened (gave birth) then you will have no trouble. Close the stanchion. Be sure there is something, hay or grain, to keep her occupied and happy.
2. Bend down and wash off the udder and the teats with a wet (if possible, warm) cloth to remove any manure or contamination. A little disinfectant on the cloth will help.
3. Move to the right rear of the cow. Let her know you are there with a light slap on the rump and by talking to her. Sit on your three legged milking stool and press your head firmly against the cow's side–this is nice and warm on a cold morning.

4. Put your milk bucket on the ground a little ahead of the udder–you are trying to keep her from kicking it over with her back legs.

5. Wrap your thumbs and first fingers around two of the teats high up against the udder. Squeeze the thumbs and fingers together and then squeeze the rest of your hand together, while pulling down a little, forcing the milk out of the end of the teat. Squirt the first squirt off to one side to clean out the milk tract in the teat. Squirt the rest into the bucket. Milk one teat at a time, alternating between the two in an up and down rhythm. Be careful of her getting restless–she will kick the bucket over.

6. Keep the whole process going on all four teats–switching back and forth once in a while between teats until she dries up (or your hands give out!). The more you get out of her, the more she will produce next time.

7. Cows keep the milk up in the udder and let it down to the teats only after appropriate stimulation–in this case you handling and cleaning the udder. If she doesn't want to let it down, give her a *light* punch in the udder to simulate the calf butting her in the udder. She will let the milk down for only about twenty minutes then you will be all through even if there is still milk in the udder.

8. Milk twice a day, always at the same time if possible, seven days a week. Many European farmers milk three times a day. Dairy farmers don't get much time off! Dry her up by changing to once a day for a couple of weeks.

9. You can let her calf finish her off after you have finished milking–if you leave some, perhaps two teats for the calf.

When you have finished milking, turn her out and take the milk to wherever you have selected to take care of the milking equipment. Vet stores and feed stores in the country sell special filters for filtering milk to get any straw, or anything else that has fallen into the milk pail out of the milk. Clean and sterilize all the equipment carefully ready for the next use.

You can give any extra milk away—most states have laws prohibiting you from selling unpasteurized milk—but you can always ask for contributions to pay for the cow's feed (that isn't really selling it, is it?)

There are two types of milking machines. Large dairy farms have systems with built in piping to all the milking stalls and all the milk goes into one large container. The cleaning and sterilizing of these systems is very time consuming. There are also small one cow machines that sit beside the cow and hold all that they milk from the cow. These also take some time to clean and sterilize, but you can do it in the comfort of your kitchen.

Your milk cow can be milked for about ten months, with production declining in the last couple of months. You can get her bred while she is still milking. Get her bred after milking her for maybe three months—this will give her a dry period at the end of the gestation when the calf inside her is making more demands on her body. Or you can breed her earlier and dry her up a couple of months before calving.

Feeding the milk cow: Producing milk is hard on a cow especially if she is a good milker. Ideally she needs good, lush, rich pasture and some grain to go along with it. In winter your very best fine leafy hay should go to the calves and next best quality to the milk cows. Let the beef cattle, horses, and goats, etc. have the poorer hay—they are not giving you gallons of milk every day. Give her all the hay she wants—cows are not particularly greedy. One day you will be butchering her for meat so any gains she makes are for the best.

Housing for cattle: Cows need little or no housing. They can tolerate a great deal of cold, but do benefit from some shade in summer. Even very young calves do not really need any more than a manure-free yard.

Your arrangements for a place for milking will be up to you and will depend on the number of cows and how deeply you want to invest in the cow business.

Fencing for cattle: Abraham Lincoln earned his living in his younger years as a rail splitter. Rail fencing has almost disappeared in America–it uses up too much valuable wood and is too labor intensive.

Most fencing for cattle and horses nowadays is barbed wire. Barbed wire can be attached to wooden posts or steel posts. If you have a wood lot with suitable wood for posts then wood is cheaper, otherwise use steel posts. Wood posts must be treated chemically if they are not to rot away in two or three years. The chemicals to treat them are toxic–handle with care. Barbed wire fences have a minimum of three strands of wire, and more often four or five. Barbed wire is sold in 330 foot rolls (20 rods). Fence posts are usually spaced one rod (16½ feet) apart. The corners must be braced so that the tight wire does not pull the corner posts out of the ground–the wire is pulled very tight before fastening to the posts.

For temporary fencing electric fencing works fine. Electric fence machines come in two types–110 volt or with a built in battery. They usually have two settings: high and low. The length of wire they will energize varies with the strength of the machine and the type of wire used. One word of caution–do not use electric fence along a public highway where it can be a danger to the public. Children and people with heart problems are endangered by electric shocks. Use it for internal fencing on your own property only.

Butchering: You *can* do it yourself–it's a lot of work–good luck! I only ever did one myself and decided it just wasn't worth the effort to do it with inadequate tools and facilities. Let a slaughter house do it. In some areas there are traveling butchers who will come, with their equipment, and do the whole thing right at your place ready to go into the freezer.

A young milk cow that has had trouble with her first calf or has not been a good milk producer can be fed up to a better condition for butchering a little after being dried up and will make good beef.

The prime ages for butchering for steers are from eighteen months to twenty-four months of age. A one thousand pound steer dresses down to about 590 pounds of meat when hanging up as two sides of beef. These end up, after trimming as about 425 pounds of packaged meat. These figures will vary with the condition of the animal, the grade (choice, good, standard or commercial), the thickness of its muscle and the amount of fat.

A 200 pound calf butchered for veal gives about 107 pounds of packaged meat.

Quite often when you have an animal butchered at a slaughter house, whether is be a steer or a sheep, you will not get the hide or fleece–if you want it they may want you to buy it back off them even though it was from your animal. They take it as part of the payment for the butchering.

Oxen: As mentioned earlier, oxen are steers that have been trained to work in harness. Oxen were the work horses of the poor farmer and still are in many third world countries. Many American pioneers crossed the wide plains of our country at the heads of plodding oxen–then they were used to break the ground in new homesteads. They are strong, docile, and can be worked for fifteen to twenty years–then eaten!

Training oxen: They are started off at a very early age. One old time practice was to put leather collars around the necks of two very young calves and hitch the two collars together about eighteen inches apart. The two animals were raised and fed while being constantly attached together. After some months the attaching strap could be removed and they still remained together as though joined.

Working oxen are quite often fitted with shoes. Oxen shoes are quite different from horse shoes. Oxen have a split hoof and the shoe is in two parts.

Over the centuries a variety of methods of yoking oxen have been developed. The crudest involves simply fastening a pole to both the horns of both oxen–rendering their heads immobile. Modern yokes are the type you often see hanging on the walls in restaurants. They are a carved from hard wood to fit on the animals neck and shoulders with a loop under the neck. Oxen are not usually driven but rather are led from the front.

CHAPTER FOURTEEN

SHEEP

Nomenclature: Male sheep are rams, females are ewes, and babies are lambs.

General: Sheep are one of the easiest animals to keep in that they can be man-handled without needing a crane to pick them up. They are prolific—one breed can have litters of four or five lambs. The meat is quite low fat (if they are fed correctly)—they give a yearly crop of wool and the meat to some of us tastes better than beef or pork. On butchering they give not only meat but also beautiful warm fleeces. It is a pity that consumption of lamb in this country seems to be limited to recent immigrants and a few of religious groups.

Breeds: The most common breed in the United States is the Suffolk. Other breeds are the Rambouillet, Targhee, Columbia, Hampshire, Finn, and Polypay. Rambouillet, Columbia, and Targhee are white faced sheep that are raised for both meat and wool. Suffolk and Hampshire are black faced sheep that are raised for meat. Polypays are a multi-cross breed developed at the DuBois Sheep Station in Idaho.

One breed of interest is the Finn. Finns are quite small and have low grade fleeces. Why are they of interest? It is because they are the ones that have not just one lamb or two, but have litters of lambs. Now, nobody wants litters of small lambs, but if the Finn is crossbred with other breeds the proclivity to have more than just twins carries over into the resulting crossbreds.

The US Government has experimental stations that have spent

many years breeding better producing animals. One very success-ful result is the Targhee—named after the Targhee Experimental Station. This is a fast growing large white face breed that can handle extreme cold.

Buying: Sheep are sold as lambs (for butchering or for breeding), as open (unbred) ewes, as bred ewes, and as rams.

It is risky to buy open or bred ewes—you don't know if they are just culls. Unless you buy the whole flock, I don't recommend buying ewes. It is safer to buy ewe lambs. Lambs are normally sold at one hundred pounds of body weight—this is the butchering weight for tender lamb. Buy a ram lamb from a different flock. At one hundred pounds the ram will immediately start trying to breed any ewes that are in heat unless you keep him segregated. See breeding below.

Caring for your sheep: Sheep do need some attention. If they are living on a soft type soil or pasture, their hooves will become overgrown. In the wild sheep keep their feet in shape because they move around on all types of ground and the harder, rougher ground keeps the feet worn down. If the sheep's hooves become too long the edges of the hoof tends to turn inwards. This causes a pocket that becomes packed with soil and manure and is a breeding ground for disease. It is necessary, at least once a year, to trim off the excess growth with a hoof knife. Sheep are fairly docile and immobile once you get them in a position where the front of the body is up off the ground and they are sitting on their tails.

Sheep with long tails have problems with fly eggs being de-posited under the base of the tail and maggots multiplying there. The tails should be docked off at about one inch length. The sim-plest way is with the rubber band method as outlined previously in the section titled "Castration" in the Chapter on Cattle. The tail will fall off in a couple of weeks.

Old ewes can have problems with their teeth. It happens that they can loose teeth and can end up with a set of teeth that do not properly bite off grass and hay. Sometimes we want to keep such an older ewe longer than normal because she is such a good mother and has multiple births of nice lambs. If you have several in this category, talk to your vet about removing teeth to enable them to eat properly.

The thick wool fleeces of sheep are a home away from home for many parasites, such as sheep ticks, etc. The sheep need to be dipped, and that means completely submerged or completely sprayed, with commercial sheep dip. Do it at least once a year Spray any new animals you get before they mix with your clean stock.

Breeding: Gestation for lambs is from 144 to 151 days, however some individual ewes may go as few as 138 or as many as 159 days. Ewes are seasonal breeders and normally only come in estrus (heat) in the fall and have their lambs in the spring. The onset of the estrus is affected by the decreasing length of the days. It pays to try to get them bred as early as possible in the fall for early spring lambs. Ideally you want your lambs born as soon after New Year's Day as possible so as to reach a decent size by Easter. Lamb prices are highest just before Easter. Many religious groups traditionally serve lamb at Easter and lamb big enough to butcher is in short supply at that time. For those of you farming near a cosmopolitan city there can be a good market for lamb. The price slumps quite severely after Easter. Some religions want to buy the lambs live.

There are chest strap contraptions that you fasten around the ram's chest that contain a staining mixture. This is so a colored stain is left on the ewe's back after the ram mounts her. As each ewe is marked, move her to a different pen or field so the ram can concentrate on the ewes that have not yet come into heat. He will check out each ewe daily and only breed the ones that are in heat. If you are using more than one ram, use different colored stains in the chest contraptions. If you have any identifying system for the ewes (usually some form of ear tag) you can keep track of the date each was bred and the ram that bred her. You will know when to pen her into her own private pen to lamb some months later This system also lets you identity the ewes that are not going to lamb because they did not get bred. After he has bred all, or almost all, the ewes, let him at them again in case some of the breedings didn't take and the ewes come in heat again.

Lambing: Ideally each ewe has her lamb(s) (hopefully she will have more than one) in a nice private pen all by herself. This gives her an opportunity to bond with the baby. Even in large flocks there are attempts to do this by putting each ewe in a four foot square pen to lamb and for a couple of days after. Sheep, unfortunately, have a tendency to reject any lamb with which they have not immediately bonded.

Ewes can have problems when lambing. Like calves, lambs should be born head first with the front legs tight against the side of the head. Sometimes it is necessary to reach up into the ewe and turn the unborn lamb around or help it be born–particularly if there are twins or triplets and they are going to be breech births. A person with a small hand (like my wife) can do this quite easily and save some lives. Make sure the ewe gets to smell and lick the lamb *immediately* to prevent rejection of the lamb. At this time it is sometimes possible to graft an orphan lamb on to a ewe–they are not very bright animals. If the ewe's lamb is born dead or dies, rub the dead lamb's body on an orphan to fool the ewe with the smell of her own lamb.

Raising lambs: Like all mammals, lambs thrive on their mothers' milk. At a month or so old they are ready to start eating some high protein feed and some high quality hay. Put the feed in an area with a narrow gate that the ewes cannot get through.

If you will want to replace any of your ewes with new ewes, tag the lambs that were from multiple births (twins and triplets). These are more likely to have twins or triplets themselves than are the lambs of ewes that had just one lamb. Also keep track of the fastest growing young ewes–these are also good candidates for keeping.

Orphan lambs and lambs rejected by their mothers can be quite successfully raised on bottled milk substitute. Use the same kind of bottle used for day old calves, but with a much smaller nipple. Give them all they want to drink. Wean them as soon as it appears that they can get along eating grain and hay.

The idea on raising lambs is to have them early in the year and grow them as rapidly as possible to catch the high spring prices.

Castrating: Male lambs are castrated using the rubber band method–the same as the tail docking above. Castrate them anywhere between two weeks and two months old. After that they may try to breed the ewes.

Selling lambs and older sheep: At the time to sell the lambs– at about 100 pounds, pick out the ones that you will want to keep. If possible sell your lambs directly to the public and cut out the profit taken by the supermarkets. You can take orders and have a lamb butchered and packaged for your customers. Right now the price of lamb chops and leg of lamb in the supermarkets is astronomical!

Older sheep, when butchered, make mutton. Many people, including myself, do not like the strong taste of mutton. You can send them off to the auction yard, but don't put a reserve price on them–they will only bring a couple of dollars each. There just is no demand for older sheep.

Shearing: Sheep are sheared in the spring before it gets too hot.

Sheep shearing on large sheep farms is done by professional shearers who travel from farm to farm shearing for so much a head. It takes a lot of wool to fill one of the enormous burlap bags that are used for raw wool. They will not come to your place to shear a handful of sheep. If possible make arrangements to truck your sheep to a farm where they will be shearing a lot of sheep and get them to do yours while they are there. See if you can join a wool pool.

You can shear them yourself using hand or electrical shears. There is quite a skill in doing a decent job of shearing a sheep, but it can be learned. Some small farmers keep the more rare breeds of sheep and sell the wool to hobbyists who spin and weave the wool into handmade garments, etc.

Housing: Sheep need little or no housing. A place to get out of the wind in the worst winter weather is really all they need. With their heavy coats, they do need to be able to find some shade in the heat of a summer day.

Butchering: A one hundred pound lamb will dress out to two hanging halves of about 48 pounds of meat which will make a total of about 38 pounds in packaged meat. Check the price of lamb in the store and you will see that raising lamb can be quite profitable.

CHAPTER FIFTEEN

GOATS

Nomenclature: Male goats are Bucks (or sometimes called Billy goats), females are does, and young goats are kids.

Breeds: Nubian, Toggenburg, Saanen, Alpine, and LaMancha. Angora goats are raised for their hair–mohair.

Breeding: Goats should be bred at 8 months of age when they weigh about 80 pounds. The gestation period is 150 days.

Milking: Due to their smaller size, goats are milked while standing on a platform three to four feet high. There is a good demand for goat milk at a good price in many hospitals. Due to the smaller size of the fat particles in the milk, goat milk is easier for premature babies to digest.

Feeding, butchering, and general care of goats differ very little from that for sheep.

CHAPTER SIXTEEN

RABBITS

Raising rabbits is not a "get rich quick" scheme, but can be profitable as a small farm enterprise or even a full time occupation, if good management is practiced and attention is paid to details. A rabbit has the greatest reproductive potential of any farm livestock. A doe can produce up to 10 times her weight in edible meat in a year's time. Rabbit meat is easy to digest and naturally low in fat and cholesterol.

Before raising rabbits, you need to make sure there is a market for the product. A family can consume the production of a small rabbitry, but larger enterprises require a consistent year round market to be successful.

Angora rabbits are raised for their hair, for spinning and weaving.

In addition to the sale of meat, there is some demand for rabbit fur. The tanned pelts can be sold as is or turned into such items as women's purses, gloves, etc.

Nomenclature: A female rabbit is a doe. A male is a buck. Baby rabbits are kits. A fryer is a 4-6 pound rabbit, less than 14 weeks old, sold for meat consumption. A roaster is any rabbit over 6 pounds and over 14 weeks old sold for meat consumption. A doe delivering young is said to kindle.

Housing: many types of housing can be used for rabbits. Housing must provide sufficient protection from weather extremes; rabbits suffer more from heat than from cold. Housing must also provide protection from predators, wildlife and other disturbances to the rabbitry. Rabbits require excellent ventilation to be productive and stay healthy.

Wire cages placed inside a shed or pole building are the most common type of housing. The wire cages should have a wire bottom of ¼ inch mesh, but one quarter of the cage should have a solid bottom for the animal to rest on to prevent wire burn on the rabbit's legs. Usually this is a piece of one by six or one by eight lumber about twelve inches long. The rabbits will chew on the wood and it will need replacing from time to time.

A doe with a litter should have a 30 inch by 30 inch cage, 18 inches high. Other cages are required for growing out fryers, for bucks, for junior does and to isolate sick animals.

Nest boxes protect young rabbits. A typical nest box is 12 inches high, 12 inches wide, and 18 inches long. One end has 6 inches open at the top to permit entry of the doe and to prevent the kits from getting out. A doe normally does not stay with her young; she only enters the nest box to feed them. A partial lid provides additional protection and allows access to the box. The nest box goes inside the doe's cage a couple of days before she is due to kindle.

Breeds: While there are over 50 breeds of rabbits recognized and many varieties of those, the medium breeds such as the New Zealand White and California are the most suitable for commercial rabbit meat production. Medium breeds mature at 9 to 11 pounds and produce large litters that yield good quality carcasses. Giant breeds (12 pounds and over), such as the Flemish Giant or Checkered Giant, are suitable for cross breeding, but should not be used in their pure form due to their lower meat to bone ratio.

Buying rabbits: The best place to buy rabbits breeding stock is from a reputable breeder who can show records that attest to the performance of his herd. Good quality stock can often be purchased at state and county fairs. It is best to start small and grow gradually into the rabbit enterprise.

Feeding rabbits: Rabbits need clean, fresh water to be available at all time. The best method is to use sipper type bottles that are hung outside the cage with the metal sipper tube inside.

Feed is the largest single cost in rabbit enterprise. It takes about

15 pounds of feed to produce a 4 pound fryer. Most rabbit producers feed commercial rabbit pellets; these meet all the rabbit's nutritional needs and can be purchased at most feed stores. Purchasing in bulk can result in substantial savings.

Rabbits are finicky eaters and are sensitive to sudden changes in feed. You should discriminate against feed that is dusty and has too many fines (powder). Pellet size is important–you don't want a pellet that is too large or too small. Quality will vary between brands and batches of rabbit pellets.

Ideally there are four rations that should be fed, based on the rabbits' requirements. Realistically only one ration is fed and this should be 16-18 percent crude protein. Care must be taken not to overfeed rabbits. Fat, lazy rabbits are difficult to breed.

Feed daily in the following amounts:

For growth: 5-6 oz

For maintenance of size: 4-6 oz

During gestation: 4-6 oz early in gestation and gradually increase to free choice.

During lactation: Free choice (give does 2 tablespoons of whole corn daily for the first three weeks of lactation

Breeding: Most rabbits are ready to breed when they are 5-6 months of age. The doe will be larger in size and mature one month earlier than the buck. One buck for every ten does is the recommended ratio. Bucks should be used once a day, but can be used more often for a limited time.

Rabbits do not exhibit an estrus (heat) cycle like other animals. Ovulation (egg release) takes place 10 hours after copulation (breeding).

A doe can produce up to 8 litters a year, depending on the re-breeding schedule and management skill of the breeder. The doe should be taken to the buck's cage–does are aggressive and territorial; the two should not be left alone. Mating should occur immediately. If the mating is successful the buck will generally snort and fall to one side. The doe should be bred twice before being returned to her cage. Some producers prefer to return the doe to the buck's cage 8 to 12 hours later for the second breeding.

Gestation period for rabbits is 30 to 32 days. The nest box should be placed in the doe's cage 28 days after mating. Straw should be used as the bedding material in the nest box. The doe will pull hair from her chest and abdomen to line the nest. Within 24 hours after kindling (giving birth) the nest box should be examined and the afterbirth and any dead or deformed kits removed.

Average litter size is 8 to 10. Kits are born blind, hairless and deaf. The doe nurses them generally only once a day, for only about 3-4 minutes. Kits can be transferred to another doe to equal out the size of litters if there are no more than three or four days difference in the ages of the kits.

Kits will grow hair by four days old and open their eyes at 10 days of age. The nest box should be removed when the kits are three weeks old and spending most of their time outside the nest box.

The doe's milk production will start to drop off at about three weeks and the litter can be weaned at four weeks of age or later if an immediate re-breeding is not wanted.

By 8 to 10 weeks of age most fryers will weigh at least 4 pounds and by 12 weeks 4.5 pounds—ready for market.

Health: Rabbits need few medications when compared to other farm animals. Good sanitation, proper ventilation and regular observation are the keys to maintaining a healthy and productive herd.

Butchering: Use a piece of metal pipe or hardwood about ½ inch diameter and some nine inches long to stun the animal. Pull the ears forward and strike a quite hard blow to the back of the neck, at the base of the skull; this will stun and sometimes kill the animal. Immediately hang the carcass by its back legs and cut the throat let it bleed out for a few minutes.

Cut around the hind paws and cut from the belly cut up to the paw. Cut around the anus carefully to avoid contaminating the meat. Pull the skin down off the paws; then pull the skin off the body as though you were peeling a pair of gloves off. Pull the skin over the head and cut the head off.

Starting at the anus, cut the thin belly skin and remove all the internal organs. This is the time to decide if you want it whole or cut up. Wrap it, or the pieces of it, in freezer paper, mark the outside with the contents and the date and put it in the freezer—or take it to the stove and start cooking!

CHAPTER SEVENTEEN

HORSES–AND MULES

People keep horses for a variety of reasons: Saddle horses for pleasure; working saddle horses to work cattle or sheep; draft horses for a variety of uses; race horses; and simply because they like to see horses in the pasture behind the house!

The US Internal Revenue Service looks at any mention of horses on income tax forms with a very jaundiced eye. Evidently it is OK with them for you to declare income from horses as taxable income–that is a business and the income is taxable; but it is an entirely different thing if you try to claim losses from horses–that is a hobby and the losses are not deductible!

Nomenclature: A male horse is a stallion; a female horse is a mare; a young male horse (under 4 years old) is a colt; a castrated stallion is a gelding; a young female horse is a filly. A mule is a hybrid cross between a mare and a male donkey. Mules are prized for their strength, endurance and agility. Mules are sterile.

Breeding, raising and training of horses are outside the purview of this book. Raising, breeding, feeding, castrating of horses is not a great deal different than that of cattle. The training is a specialized business and, at least in this country, we do not butcher them for meat.

Farming with horses and mules: In the southern states small scale farming with mules and horses has never died out. And in the Northwestern United States–Oregon, Washington, Idaho–it is even being re-introduced for larger farms. What is the main advantage to using horses instead of a tractor? As one older man told me, "You never look out of your window in the morning and see that your big red tractor has had a little red tractor!" A good four horse hitch of large work horses and the necessary harness can be bought for much less than a new tractor and they can do an awful lot of work–without paying the price of gasoline or diesel fuel–you can grow the fuel that they use: grass, hay and a little grain! A major problem with horse farming is the availability of horse drawn machinery. None has been made since the 1940s and that is now rare and worn out. There are methods of adapting tractor machinery for horse use that involve using a kind of chariot between the horses and the machinery. Farming with working horses is a specialized business. If you have to buy the feed for the horses due to insufficient pasture in summer and have no hay of your own for the winter then it is probably best to forget about horses–big horses have big appetites. There are numerous sources of information about farming with horses—I just checked on an Internet search engine for "draft+horses" and came up with 6756 pages of web sites! There are specialized magazines and books on the subject–check with www.amazon.com.

Foot care for horses: A horse is only as good as its legs and feet. Horses hooves need care. The hard outer layer needs to be kept trim and even. The soft frog in the center of the hood needs occasional trimming. Compacted manure and dirt needs to be cleaned out of the hooves on very regular basis.

Horses being used regularly need shoeing. You can do this yourself, but it is a fine skill to do properly. This level of care is best taught to you by a farrier or a vet who specializes in horses.

CHAPTER EIGHTEEN

OTHER LIVESTOCK

Fish and fish ponds: I know of a gentleman, a friend of ours, living near Spokane, Washington, who had a very small, clean, stream running through his property. He excavated three ponds along the course of the stream. He hatches fish eggs out in small building, also with the same water running through it. With suitable wire mesh barriers; he raises trout in the three ponds at a very nice profit.

Way out in desert, near Tucson, Arizona, there is a man who excavated a large pond in the desert dirt. He lined it with plastic sheeting and raises tons of shrimp every year—at over seven dollars a pound for organically raised shrimp, with none of the pollutants now found in ocean shrimp, he is doing very well!—salt water shrimp in the middle of the Arizona desert!

In the southern United States there are many quite profitable fish farms raising that southern delicacy, catfish. Many are a part of a restaurant set up, but some sell frozen fish and also sell directly to the public.

Bees and bee hives: Bees make a very nice sideline for any farm. Other than some sugar water occasionally, they feed themselves, breed themselves and raise their young themselves—you just get to harvest the honey.

It would probably be smart to get yourself and all your family checked for allergic reaction to bee stings before getting into bee raising—no matter how much protective gear and how careful you are you will get stung once in a while.

Bee hives can sometimes be rented out as pollinators in such places as orchards and other crops that rely on bees for pollination—you get paid and the pollen feeds your bees—what a great deal!

Bee keeping is another one of those skills that are best learned from an expert. Try to find someone to give you a hands on guided tour before you invest any money in hives and queen bees.

CHAPTER NINETEEN

CONCLUSION

In the first five chapters of this book I have tried to outline some of the considerations, expenses and problems that can be encountered when a city/suburban family moves to the country. I strongly recommend that you re-read them and do not try to whitewash the things that you must consider before making such a move. Moving from the pavements and sidewalks of the city to the dirt roads and mud of the country can be a traumatic change. It is particularly difficult for the lady of the family who may no longer have access to such conveniences as laudromats and a supermarket one block away. The children may be moving from a school with ten or more classrooms of the seventh grade to a seventh grade class of ten children; from a school with thousands of students to one of maybe only one hundred students. They will have fewer opportunities for choice in their schooling since there will be fewer elective classes.

Butchering livestock that you have raised yourself can be a difficult at first; some people never can learn to kill something that they have named.

The essence of farming is patience. The patience to wait for a crop to grow, for animals to grow and reproduce. And the fortitude to realize that sometimes nature and the weather do not co-operate and the crops can fail; animals can be barren and can die.

Money is a major consideration. Unless you have a lot, and I do mean a lot, of money to invest, it is extremely difficult to make a living farming. Good land is expensive and machinery costs are becoming prohibitive. Every year hundreds of experienced farmers and ranchers go out of business or go bankrupt. Consumers in the United States get the best food in the world at extremely low prices compared to other western countries. They get those benefits because of the extreme competition that exists. The United States produces more food than we can eat and this drives prices down—good for the consumer, but not so good for the producer.

Think about spending a vacation on one the farms that advertise farm vacations—if you do this, try to find a place that has both animals and crops. It might help you to make a decision about that major change in your life.

Think about taking college courses in such subjects as soil management and animal husbandry. Learn about plumbing and electricity. Take a course in welding—your machinery will break down. Learn auto and truck repair. Tour a slaughter house. Do anything and everything you can to prepare yourself and your family for the move.

I have tried in this little book to outline some of the possibilities for you to consider. Get on the Internet and research the things that attract your interest. There is vastly more information available nowadays than I could ever put in this book.

Good luck in your move to the country!
Dennis Ogden